18 Months

Claire Sheffi

This book is dedicated to my beautiful and inspirational boys, Alex and Max, you make my life whole. And to my Grandad who gave me faith.

It is also dedicated to all individuals who dare to dream of a life beyond what you currently have. Hold on with all your might!

Spring

A journey, in my opinion is seldom straight forward, or an easy path underfoot. This part of my journey began in January but truly sprouted new shoots in Springtime. At times I feel like a cat that has lived eight of its nine lives and is clinging onto the last one so that it truly counts. I think as humans we often behave like we have more than one life to live, that this gift of precious time is a given, taken for granted, instead of treasured. What crazy fools we are to be caught up in this chaos of false certainty. This story is one of daring to dip a toe and then a foot and finally fully submerge into a life dream. This story doesn't start at a logical beginning, but at a pivotal point where the spinning top is going so fast you can't see the delicate pictures that decorate the metal body. It starts with spinning. It starts with a removal van and the keys to a little slice of heaven.

*

I moved to my little cottage almost five years ago and despite many tears being shed over that period, I've never looked back. I found myself one January sat with my Dad who had come up to visit for my birthday, looking through properties for sale. Not for me, but for him, he was curious regarding what prices were like 'up

North'. While scrolling he stumbled across a darling little cottage that had a beautifully long garden, which backed out onto an uninterrupted view of fields and the moors. I was immediately taken in by the charm of this diamond find. Not once during this scrolling moment did it occur to me that I would be occupying it just a few months later!

At the time I was married and living in a local village. Despite being very much in love with my other half, it would appear that he was more in love with himself and his unfaltering narcissistic behaviour than with me. I'm not going to dwell too much on this moment in time, simply because it doesn't deserve the attention. What I can safely say is that my heart was breaking due to his behaviour, and shortly after my Dad returned home the bottom fell out of my marriage completely. I was now sitting in a cold cellar looking for a new home.

While looking for options that were in my price range, I once again stumbled on the little cottage and figured it was time to take a look. I booked a viewing on a wild and wet February day and made my way to this tiny hamlet which, I now call home. I parked at the bottom of the row of terrace cottages, all blackened by time and industry. I left my car tucked into the dry stone wall overlooking the fields and made my way up the street. I didn't rush and while walking I was overwhelmed with this sense that I was coming home for the first time in a very long time. The tiny 250 year old street is built on a small hill, the cottage I was going to view was tucked away right at the very top. I slowed my pace some more, wanting to savour this moment that I felt was somehow important, and then there it suddenly was. Home. There was no gate out front, just a gap in the dry-stone wall, much of which was missing. I peered through the windows, which were badly in need of replacement, into the tiny space inside. The cottage had been empty for 18 months, I could immediately see the potential and my heart begin to sing for the first time in a long while.

The Estate Agent arrived late, and let me into, what can only be described as 'a little slice of heaven'. He didn't need to sell the place; my heart had been taken before I even crossed the threshold. I was drawn towards the patio doors which gave the amazing view of the Yorkshire landscape beyond the garden. The garden, however, was essentially part of that landscape, in the sense that it was a truly overgrown field. Mother Nature had certainly claimed it back as hers but it was clear to see that under mounds of grass there would be endless possibilities when it came to creating the perfect cottage garden. Little did I know how much of a mess actually sat beneath the grass!

I wandered around the space; it didn't take long since it truly was the smallest house on the street. The kitchen was a classic cottage style, with a tiny butlers sink. I stood holding onto the porcelain, looking out of the window towards the fields and decided that washing-up had never been so attractive! I also felt hope for the first time in a long time. The stone fireplace had amazing character, with the exception of the ugliest 1980's gas fire plonked in the middle. Nothing was putting me off! Upstairs the two bedrooms had exposed beams, and the traditional deep windows that come with cottages of a certain age. I was sold, it really was that simple!

Over the next 48 hours offers were given, then rejected and then given again. Finally we settled on a price and this 'little slice of heaven' was about to become mine. I visited 4 times before moving in, took the Man-child and Man-cub, along with a couple of friends and my Grandad. The general consensus was, that I was mad taking on this place, but they too could also see the charm.

The next few months dragged and felt more like years. The only thing which kept me going was selling as many belongings as I could from my old house so that I could invest in my new home. In my mind I mapped out where everything would go, measured and visualised all the possibilities. Moving dates got delayed and more tears were shed but I knew the end was in sight. On the fourth of May I collected the keys and with a close friend loaded my tiny Fiat to the brim, then made my way home. The removal men, who may well have had their fair share of drugs, helped me in with boxes and mountains of stuff. After everyone left, I sat on the back step with a glass of fizz, sun shining and a sea of buttercups creating a carpet of yellow in front of me. This was it. I was here. My next chapter had begun. Five years on and my heart still swells with gratitude every day and most of my world revolves around this delightful place. Its home after all, safe, secure and full of love. Little did I realise that this was just the beginning of a very different journey.

*

How often do you slow down enough to give gratitude? I don't necessarily mean to a person, more a case of throwing it out there and saying that appreciation out loud. I find myself often looking up at the sky, and saying 'thank you, thank you, thank you' because I simply feel full with hope with where my life is right now. I've seen a few springs come and go in the cottage, and my endless delight continues. The power of thanks has long been played out in different experiments, there is a classic one that anyone can carry out. Take three jars and half fill them with rice, any type of rice so long as it's all the same sort. Add water, and leave it. The next thing you need to do is start to pay attention to one of the jars of rice, say amazing things to it and nurture it. The second jar you speak to like it's a piece of shit, you are the worse version of yourself, don't hold back! The third jar you completely ignore, it gets nothing, no acknowledgement, no love, just an empty void. After four weeks open the jars and smell the rice. What do you notice? What do you see? The jar of rice that was given nurture thrived, it did well, the water smelled fine, sweet almost. The jar that was given hate went mouldy, the water smelt foul and the one which was ignored didn't fare much better either. When I came across this simple and bizarre experiment I did feel dubious to say the least. Irrespective of whether it works or not doesn't really matter in my mind. I've been watching the world and people around me of late and see an increase of demand, pace and impatience. With this comes a lack of gratitude, nurturing and kindness. I do wonder where this world of speed will take us and my ever need to escape it continues to rise.

When I'm in the garden I feel genuinely amazed that with some help, I have created this haven. I feel gratitude for the life of what my fingertips are touching. I dig and carefully put in plants that in mid to late summer will attract so much wildlife, from bees to butterflies and feed the birds that eat them. It makes my heart swell with pure joy to simply sit and watch, listen, smell and even taste this magic that is happening right in front of me. I feel hope of what is to come, what will grow with care and love.

Today I was up like a lark and in the garden at 8.30am – not bad for a Sunday. Moving plants, pruning, feeding and marvelling was all part of my few hours out there. Plants that have stayed dormant over winter, stocking up all their energy ready for new growth in spring are now starting to say hello again. The bird song and migrating birds fill the air and the grass is getting ready to explode back to its majestic self once again. I know soon the surrounding fields will be filled with buttercups creating a carpet of yellow, dusting my legs when I wander through them. The joy. The gratitude!

After a potter in the garden, I felt the need to continue to maximise the weekend, I'm becoming increasingly aware that I'm shoehorning activities into the limited weekend hours. I grab a pork and black pudding pie from my bright red fridge and eat it without consideration and head out on my bike. I'm facing into and embracing cycling the hills, which you can't escape where I live. But today was all hills, views for miles and a fulfilling sense of self grew with every stroke of the pedal. To have the best of Yorkshire as my playground makes me one hell of a lucky lass. I can't imagine living anywhere else. There has been a steady consistent rise in temperatures this last couple of weeks and with that the daffodils put on a really good show. No matter how long or short, steep or gradual the hill was today, my daffodil fan club cheered me on right to the top. I think we all have decisions to make every day, get up and embrace the world and all it has to offer or sit on the sofa thinking that the life beyond the walls is out of reach. I'm touching that life but I still feel there is something I'm not quite grasping.

The daffodils have come out to dance and encourage the new season along, I feel the same is happening on the street which I call home. Winter is now fading behind us and with it doors are opening and people are emerging from a long hibernation. One of my favourite neighbours is in hospital and at his request I need to go have a rummage in his house for fresh undies and a host of vitamin tablets. I feel unsure about this simple request at first, then I pause and consider the trust that comes with this ask for help. I ponder how pride and the ego sometimes needs to take a back seat in order to allow help in. I feel humbled. Moving onto 'the street' has been an enlightening experience and the situation with vitamins and underpants forms just part of a rich tapestry when it comes to the residents. They all slowly filtered in, one by one and have become part of the footprint on this unadopted road.

On the first viewing, me standing outside what was to become 'my little slice of heaven', I met the one who 'marches to the beat of a different drum' and entered into a friendly discussion. Even now I don't recall what we talked about, what I do recall was his vision through the varifocals, which made his eyes appear larger than normal. You could see that this individual would have been quite an attractive person once , in their heyday. I'd say 6ft tall, full stock of hair and physically in good shape. It's easy to see what is in front of us but to what depth do we see the person? I felt welcomed from the start and was informed that the house had been empty for 18 months now. The 'one that marches' has become a strange fixture in my life now, an unlikely friendship of rhubarb exchanges over the dry-stone wall, me keeping an eye on his comings and goings, more so because in the past five years I've seen a sad and steady decline in his health. I will come onto this later; it deserves its own shining light.

The week I moved in was reasonably quiet, sunny and beautiful. I met my next-door neighbours, a quiet family with a daughter who sings on the back porch. Lying in bed each night being sung to sleep was an unexpected pleasure. Her voice is soft and while I can't identify the lyrics, the simple sound of singing makes me feel safe in my bed. The girl's Mum has a thick stock of strawberry hair, it's wild, untamed and the same goes for the hair above her upper lip. Despite my best efforts I always find my eyes drawn to her breasts, they are humongous, loose and out of control. I mentally congratulate her for not giving a shit about the conformity of a bra. The combination of wild hair and unruly bosoms complements the uniqueness of the street. Her husband can be chatty one minute and evasive the next... especially when you take out a hawthorn hedge that was giving them privacy. They sync into each other in a way that is harmonious, the kind of harmony that comes from years of being together with very little influence from the outside world. Their Collie dog matches their family vibe with a bushy coat, cataracts eyes and a walking pace that screams 'there is no rush'.

Towards the end of the first week, I was sitting on the wall outside of 'my little slice of heaven', for no other reason than a blown electrical fuse. My friend Graham and his wife had come up to help install a curtain pole, at this point in time I didn't have the right tools. What should have been a simple job turned into a fiasco that lasted days. The electric cables most certainly didn't run where you would predict, Graham had drilled through the main cable and I now had no electricity. The bang was deafening and my panic immediate and so there I sat on my dry stone wall fighting back tears when two ladies came walking up the street, with what can only be described as purpose. I had this sinking feeling where I wondered if I might have blown out the electricity for more than just my house! Luckily, I wasn't in trouble, the ladies had just come up to say hello. I got yet another warm welcome to the street.

One of the ladies, who I will call 'Box of Frogs', because she is as mad as that, has entertained me and offended me in almost equal measure over the past five years. Being in her mid to late 60's doesn't stop this larger than life woman from going out and having crazy adventures that you would link normally to teenagers. During my first winter when the first big snow arrived, we were confined to the area by 5ft drifts, unless you ventured out on foot and were prepared to battle the elements. I received a knock at my door at around 11am, sledge in hand and asking if I was 'playing out'; this was and is one of my favourite winter memories from the street. While I didn't play out that day, I did watch a handful of the most mature residents from the street sledding down the hill at the back of my cottage, there was a noticeable lack of children around and the ones who did brave it looked on in fascination. I believe that the handful of people on the hill that day were all over 60, all laughing and all filled with the delightful joy of 8 year olds.

A couple of days after the sledging episode, 'Box of Frogs' knocks at my door and asks me if I want to go build and igloo. As tempted as I was, I declined, more because I was working from home and would feel guilty if I dared to move away from being present online. This is one of my life regrets, I should have gone instead of investing my time in a faceless company. It was reported back later by a slow building rumour on the street that my neighbour had taken down her shower curtain to build a shelter, made a decent enough igloo and was found with a portable stove brewing up! A golden moment if there ever was one.

By the time we entered into June I had also met a delightful lady who most certainly is not from this neck of the woods. Beautifully spoken and quite frankly, in Yorkshire terms 'posh' I was walking down the street on this uneventful morning, sun shining with me about to head out on my bike for a quick cycle. It was 10am on a Monday, that much I do remember, when 'Posh' came out of her rose clad cottage waving her arms at me. "Darling, darling", I look around wondering who the on earth this is directed to? "Darling, cocktails at six, don't be late". And so on this particular Monday in June I found myself sitting in a shaded garden with a martini in hand, listening to her fascinating life story of love, betrayal and antique dealing. A tour of the cottage with her fitting description of the 'butch pink' bedroom and smoking room lean-too made me warm inside. I staggered back up the street a couple of hours later. There was no doubt at all that I simply needed to go to bed and sleep off the cocktails, the sound of her laughter and stories were taken to bed with me.

Nettle spraying seems to be a thing if you own land and want to look after it. The next character is quite simply the fittest 90 something year-old I know and is the proud owner of the most unruly eyebrows I've ever seen! They are big, bushy and dominate his face. We met over the dry-stone wall at the bottom of my garden, he was spraying, I was wondering how I was ever going to tackle my mess of a garden. 'Eyebrows' and I would have some grand conversations in the months that followed, most involving him being amused by my antics and me soaking up the stories he would tell me about the street. One particular day he decided to tell me about Septic Cyril, who used to live in my little slice of heaven many vintages ago.

Cyril came into our conversation by chance, my endeavours to create a beautiful cottage garden were becoming increasingly testing. Me with a pickaxe, generally covered in mud while navigating the mystery of what laid beneath the grass covered mounds. The garden is split level and at the very bottom end it would seem there had been two green houses, which had been knocked down and left for nature to reclaim as her own. I didn't know this until I started digging, with growing frustration and an ever expanding pile of glass. I eventually plucked up the courage to ask Eyebrows what he knew about the cottage. This question was like entering into a Narnia type wardrobe of adventure and understanding. Stepping through into a world of understanding allowed me to grasp why my digging efforts were becoming increasingly difficult. It transpired that Septic Cyril had carpeted the garden with a lovely thick red carpet! I like to imagine that Cyril had dated a true glamour puss of a woman and needed to serenade her with a red carpet. This, in my mind was to make his efforts of guiding her down the garden path more tempting, a bit like Adam and Eve with the apple. Once there he would proudly show her his greenhouses and the rest would be romantic history. I came to learn that no such thing would of ever happened to Septic Cyril.

He was called Septic Cyril for a reason, and while I can't fully remember how he left the street, what I do know is that when the police came into the house to remove him, one walked straight back out and vomited on the unmade road. Legend has it that it took a tractor and trailer and some strong stomached helpers to shovel the shit out of the house before carting him off too. Eyebrows told me about the day he was coming home and saw Cyril attaching a double wardrobe to the outside of the house, over the front door. There was a lot of banging, nailing, drilling and adjusting, but once finished it would seem Septic Cyril had made himself a front porch. For practical reasons, only known to Cyril, the rod with hangers were left in the 'porch' so that guests could hang their coat before entering. Cyril didn't stop there. Perhaps Cyril was the true creator of Narnia? The following day he was found with a saw in his hand fitting a letterbox into his newly built extension...

Further down the street is the man with the straw hat, yellow t-shirt and blue shorts. He collects cats and wears the same outfit from spring through to autumn. Once the weather cools substantially his winter attire comes out. Khaki cargo pants and a khaki fleece, occasionally a bobble had if the weather is fierce. In the first few weeks of me taking up residence, Straw Hat had given me plenty of tomato plants, he has a passion for tomatoes, collecting wood and cats. My passion seems to be killing tomato plants with great success much to the dismay of this kind chap. Straw Hat has lived on the street his entire life, as did his mother and grandmother. Residents remember his grandmother well, a tiny Victorian lady, who dressed in floor length skirts until the day she died. The echo is still there for those who knew her well.

The street at the time was a rough unmade road and the residents decided to club together and have it smartened up. This practice still takes place even now, with £5 donations needed to fill in potholes and general repair. When the street was being dressed for the first time, some neighbours declined the request to contribute, which resulted in a rather bizarre act of defiance from the rest of the residents. Cars were becoming far more commonplace and parking on the street was becoming a 'thing'. Any resident who declined contribution would find that their car had been tarmacked round, leaving them with a rough unmade gravel section of road and a reminder to the rest of the street that they were 'tight bastards'.

The cottages are old, up to 250 years it is said, the majority still have wood burning fires. Eyebrows was telling me about Bill, another former wood collecting resident who also happened to be a pyromaniac. Bill would often be found wandering the fields collecting anything and everything, so that he could build a fire. When Bill expired and the house was entered for the first time in a long time, it's said that it was nothing but a shell. He had taken every floorboard out and burnt the lot. There was just a stone staircase leading to what would have been the first floor.

Across the way from me are an older couple who have a greenhouse in the sky. They have built a greenhouse that is one story up with a walkway underneath. The purple haired resident used to live further down the street, but her then husband ran off with another woman to play the banjo in France... never to be seen again. And so she shacked up with an old rocker who wears the same mothballed clothes, cap, saggy pants and checked shirt every single day.

The daughter of Eyebrows lives in one of the very higgledy piggledy cottages that is intricately sandwiched with 3 others, to the point where you are never quite sure where one cottage starts and the other one stops! Access to the daughter's cottage is through a stile and into the field before you are met with the front door. Inside this cottage is a collection of jugs. Think of jugs, all ages, sizes, colours and usage. The house, like all houses on the street, is chaotic and screams 'home'. In the same set of sandwiched cottages is Mr Dissertation, I have given this thin angular chap this title because for the first three years of living here it is all he talked about. He's physically all sharp edges and would benefit from a good chip butty. The cottage has a blue door, I can't help feeling he still lives with his parents but I could be wrong...

If you pass through the stile and turn left you are met with yet another front door. The door leads into a mismatched one bedroom cottage that again is part of the intricate tangle of houses. The resident is grey in complexion, tall and is losing the battle with his combover. His more salt than pepper hair is thinning and his denial of this is displayed for all to see. He works in the city and leaves at 7.25am each day. I know this because he looks in my living room window and waves as he passes. Roughly 12 hours later the act is repeated as he makes his way towards the stile and into the confines of his home.

The house with the blue plaque is home to a parrot and a very noisy westie dog. The people who belong to the parrot and dog are an interesting pair. In the four years I've been here I have never seen Blue Plaque man smile. There is a dryness in his humour and the zest for life is either so long gone or perhaps it was never there to begin with? His wife is petite, chatty and comes and goes around the demands of her work schedule. Blue Plaque man sets off to work at 4am each day. In the summer when my windows are open, I hear the click of the car door with the wing mirrors lazily opening up and then off he goes. He returns mid-afternoon, a slow methodical plod up the street, grey woolly cardigan on and a plastic lunchbox tucked under his arm. He addresses me in the same way each time we meet. "Now then trouble, what do you know?" To which I reply, "fuck all".

When the man with the Volvo died, the main talk on the street was of his legendary parties, which often lasted up to four days. People would come and go, sleep wherever they could and continue drinking and taking drugs until normal life had to resume. When he died, he was taken to his final resting place in the back of his beloved Volvo. There was no hearse, no fuss, just a Volvo, a coffin and one hell of a send-off party. His ex-wife now lives in the house, she slots into the street with equal madness and marvellousness, no one batted an eyelid. It's just the way it is.

The lady who owned my cottage before me had also lived on the street for many a moon, raising her two children, one of which still lives at the bottom of the row, the other just down the lane. She was known for heading out on her push iron, backpack in place and filled with cans of larger. I feel a sense of peace here and know somewhere deep down inside we are kindred spirits.

There are gay people, single people, growers of drugs, cocktail makers, herbal experts, alcoholics and yoga masters, all residing in this tiny space. There is a uniqueness, a cycle which ebbs and flows with the seasons. People still hibernate here and only start to emerge when the curlews and lapwings return to their nest. Once the bite in the air starts to give way to a hint of warmth, when the wild garlic is ready for picking and the daffodils show their friendly faces, the residents start to come out of their hiding holes once again. The exchange of sprouting seedlings starts to happen, courgettes, black Russian Kale, garlic, tomatoes and god only knows what else is gifted so we can all grow our own. Later in the summer once harvesting happens, I often come home to donated bags of plums, apples, potatoes, broccoli and courgettes on my doorstep. There is a kindness and connection here, which I believe has been lost in many other places. As I sit here writing the names and faces pop in and out of my head and I wonder what will be said of me in years to come?

*

My little slice of heaven has the lowest door frame, anyone over 5ft 7" would need to stoop to enter. The space is also wider than most traditional doors that you find now-a-days, which is great in my humble opinion. There are three small panes of glass that make up the top third of the door, the rest is solid wood. On the door is a heart made out of twigs, this heart has followed me from a house to my true home. The post box on the outer wall has the message "love letters only" written on it, in the hopes that one day I do receive a beautiful love letter. One day...

The front of the cottage is covered in clematis, it hangs over the door and surrounds the windows, which also are a very classic design. There is a bench out front, where I sometimes sit and drink my morning coffee in the spring sunshine. It's also a great spot to sit and chat to the neighbours when they pass. Let's not dwell on the outside though, come on in, wipe your feet and take a seat.

I need to make it clear that the cottage is tiny! Truly really tiny. The staircase is in front of you as soon as you walk through the door, which also opens up into the living room area. The floors are covered in rugs, it keeps the place warm and I'm less precious about mud being trekked in. There is a window seat, at the moment the Twatterdale is stretched out full tilt on it, comfortable and basking with her head resting on the pile of cushions. The curtains are thick and heavy and pool on the floor, they are so weighted and keep the warmth in during the wild and crazy winter months. Every wall is home to bookshelves, all holding books of all shapes, sizes and topics, they offer a visual curiosity that pull people in when conversation is stilted. The walls are painted in a very dark green, Studio Green by Farrow and Ball, corners disappear and there is a feeling of being enveloped irrespective of the time of year.

The fireplace is stone with an old oak beam as a mantle, it's large and I imagine that once it would have housed a full stove to cook on. The log burner is usually lit on an evening, casting a warm glow in the dark space. I can often be found on my red sofa which has paisley swirls printed on the fabric. I feel comforted by the high sides and back that closes you in and keeps you warm when the mysterious drafts move around during the depths of winter. The cushions are velvet and different colours, gold, deep reds and turquoise, these too have travelled from houses to my now home. Next to the fire is a turquoise velvet chair with a sheepskin rug on, my boys battle over who will sit there. It has an extra deep seat with down padded upholstery, the perfect reading chair. The living room is a cosy place to sit and warm yourself when the weather is biblical, but also a place to escape to when the sun is blazing. There is a coffee table which was bought second-hand and has a delightful back story to it, it too is loaded with books. A pair of carved wooden feet that would serve as an ash tray also call this place their home.

    The recess under the stairs is where an old chest of draws sits, it's heavy and collects cobwebs between the gap of the wood and wall. Family photos and an eclectic mix of alcohol sit on top of the chest, there is a lamp, brass base and topped off with the funkiest shade you've ever seen! Towards the kitchen area is my kitchen table, it's around 120 years old and has more marks and grooves in it than anything else in the house, a thousand memories have all taken place around this chunk of wood, I suspect they add to the previous tales from a lifetime ago. A heavy chunky wooden fruit bowl sits on top of the table, the hens sometimes wander from the garden and sit amongst the fruit. I'm yet to find an egg though! There are three chairs around the table, one for me and one for each of my beautiful boys.

The galley kitchen is a perfect size and I have all the space I need, I often marvel at how people have huge kitchens and how they fill them with who knows what? The fridge is bright red on the front is a magnet of Jesus, you can dress Jesus in an array of clothing while waiting for the microwave to ping, which sits on a shelf above the fridge. Coloured tiles form a backsplash behind the oven and a butler's sink makes washing up a delight because of the views across the fields. Open shelves display cups and glasses, much of which I've collected over the years. Nothing matches but it all matters and has a purpose with a story. The windowsill is deep, I keep eggs from the chickens which roam the garden, freshly grown herbs and a jar of garlic bulbs on there. There is also a jar of dried lavender for cooking, lavender scones are the flavour of the month!

Everywhere you turn there are more books sandwiched into every available nook and cranny. Random collections of art and pictures are squeezed in too, some bright and fun, others dark and brooding. On one wall sits 'Foxie', who came to live with us when the Man-child thought that buying his mum a taxidermy fox head for Christmas one year was appropriate. Foxie dresses for the season, with spring being here he is sporting a hat sunglasses and a Hawaiian garland.

Fastened to the beams above the fire is a creel to dry clothes on. This is my life saver in winter and a great way to dry herbs and flowers in late summer. To the other side of the fire is a lamp made of a silk WW2 map, that sits on an old cotton bobbin from one of the mills. I still have a rotary dial phone which baffles younger guests because they can't fathom not pressing a button. Having to wait for the dial to return to its starting position before dialling the next number in the sequence is too much for the patience of people today. I personally find the sound satisfying, it lulls me. The only other lamp is a floor lamp, passed on from a good friend. This has an emerald green velvet shade, it's fabulous and delights me no end.

Upstairs is no different, William Morris wallpaper, Blackthorn in green coats the landing. The lighting fixture at the top of the stairs dominates the space and tinkles when the wind catches it because it is made up of hundreds of tiny sliced oyster shells. My bedroom is cosy. You are met with a traditional cast iron bed loaded with pillows, down duvet and extra blankets. At either side of the bed are windows with deep set sills which house plants and are decorated with heavy floor length curtains. It's the kind of bed you get into with a favourite book and struggle to leave, especially on those wild and wet days. On the exposed beams are a chain of paper butterflies, they spin in the gentle breeze that is blowing through. A huge stained glass window resides in the corner and casts a glow of different colours from the lamp that sits behind it. More books have found their way up here into the eaves, piled high, stacked and at times collecting dust. In the summer I always have fresh flowers from the garden in random jugs and pots, to bring the outside in is a pure joy.

The Man-cub's room is smaller, cosier, again with deep walls and a painting of the last supper occupied by superheroes. The sheets are cream brushed cotton and there are always more pillows than you need. There are more shelves with more books on too. As soon as the Man-cub gets home the first thing he does is head to his room and sinks into a bed of comforting delight. Last of all is the bathroom. I sigh because it simply doesn't fit the rest of the house. It has a shower, sink and toilet. It feels modern, clinical and I miss having a tub! But for now I need to suck it up and deal with it. It's not the end of the world and I feel blessed to have such a home of delight and love.

If you come back downstairs with me, I will take you into the garden. The top patio has a pergola with honeysuckle, roses and clematis growing up each of the corners. Sitting here with the sun shining while looking across the fields is one of life's pleasures, it's where I lose time and play witness to the most stunning sunsets. Before wandering down the garden path you have to get past the herb border, which has everything from lovage to chives growing. It's a real feast in summer and salads are a treat! You can brush your hand against anything and the scent will linger on your skin. The top part of the garden has a winding path which takes you through all the traditional cottage garden flowers that put on a good show wherever you look. The ash tree offers shade, the old bench made of driftwood and railway iron gives you a place to sit, you can rest your back against the tree and feel it's slight movement.

There are three steps down to the bottom part of the garden, where apple trees grow. More shrubs offer shade and a small grass space has a firepit in the middle to keep the three of us outside longer during the long summer nights. Finally there is a large bottom patio which is home to a gypsy wagon. It is painted in traditional colours and when you climb the three steps and sit inside you have the best views over the fields. It is here that the Man-child hangs out. The stable door offers not only a dream-like vista but also the musical backdrop of birds, lambs and hidden wildlife. It really is bliss!

Nothing really matches, everything has a purpose and all of it has been collected with love. Charles Dickens once wrote "The cottage of content is better than a palace of cold splendour, and that is where love was, where all was".

Fancy a cuppa tea?

*

At times I have to pinch myself, I feel that fortunate. I adore my boys, they really are the love of my life along with my grandad. I know deep down that I've not been the most conventional mother, I hold my hands up to some truly bad choices that most certainly were driven by my heart not my head. Yet my boys forgive me, we talk about errors of judgement and dig for deeper meaning in this rich tapestry of life. The Man-cub, as we speak, is 14 years of age, 15 in July to be precise, yet his wisdom is that of an older man, more in his twilight years. He has clear blue eyes, a mop of mousey hair and bone structure which is only just starting to take shape now his puppy fat is going. He's all arms and legs and will happily spend every waking moment in his PJ's. There are days where puberty is raging, this past Saturday was an example of that. He would not engage even in the slightest of conversation, in fact there wasn't even a grunt. The cub was in his pit until late in the day, when he decided it was time to leave the safeness of his warm, carefully arranged smelly sheets and wander downstairs in the hopes for food. Luckily, his mood had shifted, but not much!

I find myself trying to adjust to this new version of my son, the boy who would have ventured down the fields in late spring to check for changes in wildlife, blow dandelion seed heads and hold buttercups under my chin to see if I liked butter, had suddenly vanished. I know I need to let him be, let him grow and fester.

When I'm taking the Cub to school, a 20-mile round trip over hills and down the Dale, we listen to carefully selected music. On this particular spring day the Cub put on a song called Hey Ya by a band called Outkast. As soon as it came on, I immediately got my groove on, until the Cub asked me if I knew what the song was about? This question took me off guard since I've never paid attention to the lyrics, the tune has always carried me blissfully along. The Cub, however, had a theory about some of the lines. 'The song is about relationships Mum, an upbeat tune with a dark underbelly'. Okay so now he had my attention. We head towards the cattlegrid before turning left down the single track road that will take us into the valley bottom. I slow down, I sense this was a conversation to be savoured.

'What I mean by upbeat lyrics and a dark underbelly is that you never quite know what is going on behind closed doors. The smiles, the social media posts, the holidays, yet deep down people can by dying inside with unhappiness'. This is deep for a Monday morning commute when a light cloud inversion splatters the valley and we have the clearest of blue skies overhead. I pull over and look into those bluer and blue eyes. He takes it deeper... 'there is a line that says, "shake it, shake it, like a polaroid picture", this is indicative of what not to do. Relationships need to be nurtured, handled with love, care and given time, very much the same as letting a polaroid picture develop. Don't shake it, be patient and let it reveal its true nature.' I find myself speechless at his interpretation of such a happy song, a song that for me no longer pulls me to dance but more to dwell on past relationship choices. We arrive at School. He hops out of the car without a care in the world and vanishes into a sea of black school uniforms. I sit in the car unable to entangle my thoughts.

On the same day, collecting the Cub at 7pm from his dads, we were once again in our groove, some crazy dance tune playing with the pair of us looking like we were having an epileptic fit in the car. I announced that I thought I may have lost my moral compass, a simple statement with all details being left out as to why. The Cub turned around and stopped mid-groove and announced that 'mum, you really haven't lost it, its 'society' that tells us what is right, what is wrong and adds boundaries into what others think is expected'. For the second time in one day I find myself dumbfounded. There was more to come, he encouraged me to nurture my untamed soul, my limitless indecisiveness and to continue to live in a way which is gregarious, as wild and free as the wind that sweeps the moors. He sees me. My boys sees ME. He also never ceases to amaze me. Maybe I haven't failed as a parent, maybe my boys see a light, a different way of living and being beyond the prescription we call life.

The evening progresses and we snuggle up on the sofa, popcorn, log fire and watching Gatsby on DVD. Despite the blue skies today, the chill in the air of the night reminds me that spring hasn't given way to summer just yet! Gatsby is playing in all the swinging glory and I made the point of asking the cub if he could ever imagine living in a house like Gatsby's, his response was 'anything can be a palace if you make it so'. I'm not sure where his insight comes from, or how he pieces together life in a way which is so profound, but he does and he does it very well. I find that I often get more depth out of conversations with my children than I do adults. I feel proud.

The Cub on love and monogamy is also an interesting reflection and one I need to share. Monogamy for the Cub doesn't necessarily make sense, it's there to fit within the societal boundaries that have been formed to keep order and restrict a sense of living free. He also believes that people rush into making a lifelong commitment, one which isn't actually true or real because we too as humans ebb and flow like the seasons, constantly changing, resting, growing and blooming. Just not always in sync with each other! He's not sure what it means to love someone, its personal and requires experience, something he admits he doesn't yet have.

This morning's show stopping comment was during a song by Bonnie Tyler, 'I need a Hero'. I connected to the line "It will take more than a Superman to sweep me off my feet", which is where I promptly announced that I could change my dating app profile to say just that. The Cub advised against this, for the one and only reason that a statement like that would attract all the narcissistic men who want a challenge and to break a woman. I was also described by my friend, as a 'meteor of a woman' today, a compliment I will never forget! Despite being perceived as a force to be reckoned with, I still don't want to attract any more narcissistic men, I've truly had enough of those! The Cub said I am a hero, it's within me and there is no external factor that can match this. I don't know how to hold these compliments especially from a 14 year old.

One of the other qualities I admire about the Cub is his ability to show his vulnerability, yes, he shows it, without shame or fear. There is a man emerging from this Cub, who will offer a beautiful friendship, partnership and love to all those who he reaches. I adore him, in ways that I could never describe because there aren't words to describe him. I can only hope that he won't have his soul tamed, his spirit dampened and his wild free heartbroken as he grows, because he is perfect right now. Right at this moment.

His older brother, the Man-Child is of equal beauty. A friend asked me the other day if I had a favourite out of two baddies, because apparently most parents do have a favourite child. I genuinely don't and this really is down to the fact that both my boys are so damn delightful in their own unique ways. I adore them for it, often beyond what I show or express. The Man-child exudes life in every fibre of his 5ft 8" frame. His height is debateable and has long been the centre of family discussions that often don't end well. We believe an inch has been added to his stature, which includes taking into account the heel on his handmade clogs and the mountain of dreadlocks that surround his beautiful face. Let's start at the top and work our way down. His hair is brown with tinges of lighter shades from where the sun has worked its magic. He has 80 dreadlocks, something which he is most proud of, they are down to his waist now and vary slightly in length. On any given day you will find feathers from the down pillows stuck in there and other more carefully selected items. There are beads, a kilt pin, colourful shades of wool wound in and a ceramic letter 'A' which I bought him. If you look harder, I'm sure you will find many other objects of interest, like a bottle opener for emergencies.

He has beautiful blue eyes, like that of the Man-Cub and facial hair that, if we were all to be honest, resembles the fine hair of a new born baby. His attempt to grow a beard has been going on for five years now, there is little more than a grazing of fluff that grows at peculiar angles. I love him for his tenacity. He has great bone structure, full lips and perfectly straight teeth. His smile is infectious. On any given day he might turn up at the cottage dressed in a patterned shirt, corduroys, braces, odd socks (not by choice), a waistcoat and burgundy handmade clogs. He has a character that oozes out of him before he has even opened his mouth. You never quite know what he's going to say... seriously you don't! Like the Man-Cub the Man-Child has a unique view on the world, the lens he looks through is often very different to that of his peer group and if I were to be totally honest, he is a square peg in a round hole living in these parts. He belongs somewhere far more bohemian, a place where his tribe of people are and his sense of belonging will come into its own. My boys and I get each other, but many people do not get us, which is fine because we get each other.

The Man-child has talents, like serious talents. He has the ability to not only memorise words to complex songs, but also sing them pitch perfect without missing a beat. The nights sat around the firepit drinking beer, wrapped in blankets, serenading the stars is imprinted in my heart and mind. His impressions from TV programs is second to none, he can pull these perfectly timed moments off at the drop of a hat and with wit that stretches like the night sky itself. He marches to the beat of a different drum and I love this about him. It's not a march, it's a groove, a dance with a song that we hear and understand but not everyone else will. He resides in a slightly different version of reality to the rest of the world, one where time is different, music is central and creativity is a must. The Man-Child has recently been making rings out of wood, truly beautiful bits of jewellery, which he continues to master through trial and error driven by his own curiosity to create. I watch closely at his dabbling, the way he works things with his hands and expands his mind.

The conversations between the cub and the child are ones to behold. They vary in depth and can range from the hilarious, to exploring aspects of life that no-one of this age should really be doing. They both see beauty in nature, but in very different ways. The child has the wanderlust that I possess, it's this itch he needs to scratch but in a way which is different to mine. He has a restless soul, one which needs to roam and be free and yet is currently confined by the 9-5pm expectations of society. It's a means to an end with him, save the money, buy the camper van and go live a nomadic existence. Do I worry about him? Of course I do. But more in a way which is different to most parents. I suspect that many parents would want their children to have 'the job', house, car, partner and to live this perfect dream that society has fabricated. I on the other hand fear that he won't scratch his itch and get caught in the web that most of the global population live in. He needs that freedom, at least until his beautiful soul is ready to plant roots and find stillness.

We often talk about our dating experiences and agree that finding a partner who fits and visa versa is a challenge. In the world of fake lashes, tans, lip fillers, camera filters and enough shite on a girl's face to stop even the hardiest skin cells from breathing, he struggles to even have a first date. He looks different, dresses differently, thinks very differently to the modified shells of women around him. It's sad that the world has produced what is becoming an expected norm and is so far removed from what nature intended. I can only hope that the Man-Child meets a barefoot, nature loving, free spirited soul that can wander as freely as his. More than anything else, I hope he finds his tribe of people where he will feel at one. I wouldn't swap either of my boys or change their unique nature for anything. I'm proud that they follow their hearts and don't conform to the wooden box lifestyle. Unconditional love.

*

Spring in the cottage is a time of renewal, a time of fresh shoots, budding ideas and change. I've always explored different concepts and been naturally curious about the direction life can take you. The idea of destiny and fate fascinate me. Is our life really mapped out by a series of choices or is there something far bigger at play? Time at the cottage has allowed me to think more, usually while digging up last years misplaced potatoes in the garden. But I still feel life is spinning too fast. The 6am rise to walk the Twatterdale through fields of mud in winter and wild flowers in summer; the trot home for a quick shower, breakfast and then the 8.30am log in. My days are spent staring at a screen, interacting with virtual people who I've never actually met in the flesh. Meetings and more meetings where outcomes never actually seem to be reached, with vitamin D deficient faces looking back at me. It all feels like nonsense.

Between working, the idyllic school run and the all essential 'big shop', I don't feel there is much time left to live, breath and be. Like an elastic band I am pulled in directions I can't quite fathom. Sometimes the stretch is so much that I feel the cracks appear in my 'rubber' and the panic sets in. Please tell me there is more to life than this? I have the dream on paper, the cottage in an idyllic setting, the well paid job, beautiful children, great friends and a scruffy dog. So why do I have this niggling feeling that something is missing, that my compass is not pointing due north and my stars are out of alignment? Instead of holding this thought and turning it over in my hands, I divert my attention by looking at a dating app. I convince myself that the answer is in a relationship and this is truly what is lacking from my life. I need a companion, a soul mate, lover, someone to share life with. I'm also foolish enough to think I will find that online.

My dates so far have been nothing short of disastrous. Having never been on a dating website I decided at the beginning of the year I would give this a go. Both the Man-Child and Man-Cub were on hand to help me, advise me and guide me through what can only be described as 'online man shopping'. Date number one stated in his bio that he's 6ft 1", works out and is down to earth. There was one fact that was correct, his height and only his height!

We meet at the arranged location and set off walking, given that date number one is 48, I was looking out of the corner of my eye and wondering if he had fabricated his age along with a few other major things, like fitness level! He asked for a flat walk, which in all fairness I thought was a little odd but figured I would go with it regardless. A quarter of a mile in and it became apparent that he was starting to limp a bit and talking while walking was a challenge. And when I say talking, he didn't actually stop, but you could see him struggling for breath with the combined action. There was no two way dialogue, just one sentence strung together into the next about himself. Two miles later and 'his' conversation continued, which mostly consisted of stuff that had happened 20 years ago, his limp also grew in severity along with the snail like pace.

I'd like to think of myself as a 'good egg', down to earth and caring, however, this date brought the worst side of me to the surface quite quickly. I can't work out whether it was the fabrication of his fitness level or the fact that he talked about himself for 2 hours. Despite me trying to justify the never ending narrative, putting it down to being nervous and out of practice, I eventually just ran out of reason. I wanted to get back to my car, drive home and lock myself in the cottage, never to come out again. This experience can't be real surely?

Being a sparkling new penny to dating I was unsure of the protocol, which takes place following a date, so I thought in situations like this it's best to do nothing. Date number one messaged that evening to say he had to go to A&E as soon as I left due to having a swollen ankle. He also said that I wasn't for him, that I wasn't the worst date he'd ever had, but I came a close second! This statement was then followed by a screenshot of his foot; I was nearly sick in my mouth at this, especially since he clearly didn't cut his toenails. Maybe this was just bad luck? Afterall thousands of people sign up to these apps so there must be some success stories out there… there must right?

Over the coming week I juggled many online conversations and found myself swiping left and right with a soulless ease. What is it with people's inability to make conversation that doesn't involve them wanting to send a photo of their jewels? Even this became a true eye opener. By the end of the month, I had decided that perhaps online man shopping isn't for me. It seems to take an unnecessary amount of time and could turn into a part-time job if I'm not careful. My boss, who has been a big advocate of my 'perusal of man' , was helping by saying that I need to 'chill' and that I'm 'fresh meat'. Lord help me now. So, I froze the account… but curiosity keeps getting the better of me.

And so, as Spring comes to a close and the year gains momentum, a smidge of reflection is happening. What do I want, really? Really… I think that having time alone has been a blessing in so many ways. I'm comfortable with myself, my little home and all the strange oddities that are in my lovely little life. Do I want to date? I'm not sure. The experience so far has been a bit odd, soulless and almost invasive. But I'm not going to give up hope of meeting someone whose jigsaw pieces will compliment mine and vice versa. Maybe I give it another go?

It's the last Sunday in May and at 8am I head out towards Malham, a stunning spot which is a pure reflection of the magnificence of the Ice Age. My 9am meet up was with a guy who looked rugged around the edges and was up for a clamber. I arrived on time (for once in my life), got the jet boiler out, balanced it carefully on a rock and brewed yet another coffee. I had the wisdom to bring homemade granola for breakfast and eat this at speed before the Belgian arrived (this is before I knew he was really Adonis). Now you have to keep in mind that my vow of never dating again is strictly in place and this was not a date! Just a new friend to go walking with, a mantra I continued to repeat over and over to convince myself that this was acceptable. That the other dates were all just unfortunate, that passing wind on a zoom call was an accident, that when another date announced he knew where the clitoris was made him proud. I won't dwell on any of these moments, after all this is a friendly walk.

He arrived with his dog and I tried to be cool. At a beautiful estimated 6ft 1", slightly longer hair, slim build and a beard, I could quite happily have melted right there and then. Damn it! My nightie is tied to my toe forever! We said 'Hi', introduced our dogs to one another with the obligatory bum sniff. While our dogs get acquainted I find my mind drifting, I would definitely like to sniff him! I pull myself quickly back to the moment and try to act cool. I always think it's one of those 'could go either way' situations but according to my fanny flutter radar the interest was most certainly there. None of this really matters because it is just a walk with a new friend.

Concentrate! We set off walking, he's got long legs, firm, perfectly hairy. Concentrate! Cute arse. Concentrate! Now I have to concentrate because the limestone is slippery from years of use (as in Ice Age) and my view is on this Adonis next to me. Did I mention that his hair curls? We walked, talked, and finally hit the head of Malham Cove and the majestic limestone pavement, which I navigated with care. He made the stone hopping look easy, I looked like a beached whale trying to get from the sand into the ocean. After the cove we headed towards Gordale Scar, at which point I needed a wee! I dived behind a drystone wall, had my pants around my ankles, when Adonis announced there were people about to come through the gate. I try not to panic. I pulled up my pants, popped my head over the wall and said I was about to pee my pants and could they wait or risk seeing my bum? They waited (smart people). The lady offered to sing while I relieved myself. I said it was fine and that they could listen to me weeing instead – which they did! And so, feeling reborn again, I emerged with an empty bladder and ready to wander down to Janet's Foss.

Janet's Foss for all its beauty was rammed with tourists. What I would give to have a moon lit bath with Adonis in this crystal-clear dipping pool. I guess though for men it's a bit different. While my boobs would take on the persona of a 21-year-old, his jewels would likely shrivel to that of an old man. I quietly giggle to myself. We stopped for a moment before continuing the walk to the Scar, where my humiliation of a climb was about to begin. Gordale Scar is a magnificent cut in the rock, with a waterfall over two layers coming down into the valley below. Adonis had suggested we climb up the Scar and I, being 'cool' naturally agreed. I also thought it might be worth mentioning my fear of heights and my concern about getting the Twatterdale up the rockface. It's not a bad scramble, but for me it's enough. We got to the bit where the scramble began and Adonis asked me if I wanted to go ahead of him. I ponder all eventualities of saying yes and going first. The size of my bum, not so toned legs, lack of stretching ability… I'm best off going second I think.

Him having amazingly long legs meant that he took the task in his stride, hoisted the dogs up by their scruffs and I stretched my chubby little legs to their limit. And up we went. The first bit was over and the second-tier waterfall was in front of us. It was worth the knee shaking moment just to see this. Standing there looking at hundreds of thousands of years of formation truly is breath-taking, almost as much as Adonis. The waterfall provided a natural shower, my mind wandered again, what a delight it would be to strip and take a joint spritz. Concentrate!

Off we climbed, higher we went until we popped right out at the top, sweaty and triumphant. We stripped a layer off and I casually checked out the moment when one layer came up under another revealing the most well-defined torso I've seen – ever! Oh now I'm in trouble because this is all I can think about. Come on woman, make conversation and stop being a bloody perv! It's the curls, the speckled grey beard, finely tuned body and perfectly placed crows' feet. I'm in trouble this time. Nightie. Toe. Nightie. Toe. I must tie my nightie to my toe.

We carry on walking and talking and decide to extend the route. The conversation feels effortless. We finally get to an old cottage, where we decide to stop and sit for a while. We lean against the warm stone walls of an abandoned farm house, the sun beating down on us and the gentle May breeze is all around. The dogs chill, we chill and I fantasise about those rather delicious lips of his! Concentrate! Out of the whole walk there was something about this exact moment, I can't put my finger on it but it will be an image imprinted in my mind forever. We finally set off walking together, eventually looping back to the cars. We awkwardly say goodbye and thank each other for a truly splendid day. I drive off leaving a pile of dry dust in my wake. It was a splendid day, a perfect date, but I know that for whatever reason I will never see him again. I also feel ready to delete the dating app once and for all.

As Spring turns into Summer my attention turns back to focusing on my niggle and not the man.

Summer

We have eased unseen through the front door of summer, where the days are long, basking in those endless daylight hours, where you feel life will go on forever. The summer solstice marks the occasion where the maximum light is squeezed out of the year, I have friends that mark the occasion with moonlight bathing, sleeping under the stars and dancing around fires. Others are oblivious, with the day passing like any other. Everywhere you look people have a relaxed air about them, the complete opposite to winter. I've tied a bow around my dating experiences, popped them into a box and figure that it's best I leave matters of the heart to other people. For me the mountains are calling, the meadows, the Yorkshire gritstone, the smell of my tent, the jet boiler and morning coffee being drank against a spectacular backdrop. My resentment of 9-5pm working is building and my pull towards a different way of living is growing. I feel there is something I can almost touch, smell and taste, its right there, closer than ever, I just don't know quite what it is yet! There is an unsettlement brewing and it won't go away. It doesn't matter how I try and distract myself, I can't seem to escape it, whatever it is? Whenever I feel like this I tend to head to the hills to think, or as it might well be, not think, just be!

*

I've not been well this past week, I've felt pretty grotty actually, but by Thursday evening I could feel the bounce back in my heels. Then the familiar itch starts, the one where I hear the Fells of the Lake District calling and my need to scratch becomes stronger and stronger. By Friday morning I know without a doubt that it is time to start pulling my kit out of draws and do a lunch hour pack, so that come 5pm I would be ready to drive. The risk of doing a solo wild camp is that if you forget anything at all you are totally buggered. It's not like you can ask a friend for an item or kit loan. I felt quietly confident that I was absolutely covered. The excitement bubbles in my stomach and my skin feels like it is alive and ready for adventure.

And off I set in my little red Fiat 500 which is carrying the all essential cargo. The Twatterdale knows something exciting is going on, she is beyond being a 'keen bean', following me around the cottage until the minute we leave. A quick stop at the supermarket to buy some whisky for the hip flask, collect any last minute bits of fruit, fill up with petrol and then off we go. I had a rough idea of where I was going to pitch for the night. I settled on Red Tarn at the back of Pike O'Blisco, which is nestled just off Wrynose Pass and also accessible from the Langdale valley. I opt for Wrynose

Pass, for the simple reason that the weather forecast was patchy and for those of you who know the mountains, things can go from being okay to a nightmare very quickly! At least if I did need to drop the tent and go at any point, access to my car would be quicker, easier and in theory less risky.

Navigating the tourist traffic is as frustrating as ever, this I eased with upbeat music and out of tune singing, I have that carefree feeling that only comes with a last minute road trip. I've not been over to the Langdale range for a couple of years and decided to take the road that leads to Dungeon Ghyll. It feels like coming home. I have one of those serious heart swell moments and my excitement triples instantly. I navigate the road from Dungeon Ghyll, over the cattle grid and up the 25% hair pin bends, which then takes you over towards Little Landale and Wrynose Pass. The twists and turns become familiar instantly, along with potholes that you could comfortably lose a small child in. The Twatterdale has gone from sitting to standing, her instinct is apparent and her excitement un-squashable. We feed off each other's energy and I promise her that we are nearly there.

Driving up Wrynose pass is just as fabulous as always, with its gradient topping out at 30%, what's not to love. Maybe it's the single track with drops that would leave you for dead if you came off the road that supports this thrill of a drive... or maybe just being surrounded by Fells that have stood the test of time in these post glacial years?. At the top I park the car next to the stone that marks the crossover of three counties. I let the Twatterdale out, who immediately is beside herself with giddiness. I check my backpack one more time, hoist it onto my back, lock the car and set off walking. I feel my body adjust to the weight and my centre of gravity shifts to compensate. The path is well marked and trodden, I'm also reasonably familiar with it and don't feel the need to use my map. The skies are a mix of greys but the summits were clear, which is always good news. There is the odd person coming off the Fells, heading back to life, while I'm about to embrace the solitude for a precious few hours.

I continued to walk at a steady pace, which is great considering the kit I'm carrying. Before long, the tarn is in sight, so is the wet marsh-like ground which surrounds it, making it less inviting to camp. What I do have my sights on is a plateau at the far end of the tarn, its elevation perfectly raised with a view over Crinkle Crags and Bow Fell that would be simply perfect! It didn't disappoint. The plateau is delightfully flat, stone free and just waiting to be camped on. I dropped my backpack and begin to pitch my tent. Luckily, there is no wind, which has made the event superfast and without issue. What I did noticed on my walk up is a lone figure standing on the adjacent fell, not really moving, just watching with a dog. This lone figure remains there for at least 45 minutes. Now I must stress, I feel safer on the Fells than I do in most towns or cities, this is the first time I feel caution because he continues to linger and watch.

Earlier in the day a friend who works for the mountain rescue said he would pop up and say hello, so I at least know I have a companion for a few hours. I've just got settled when he turns up, two-fold out chairs and a bottle of wine in tow. How perfect! I asked mountain rescue Bob about the lone figure on the hill, to which he replies, 'it's a farmer rounding the sheep up'. I felt dubious about this theory because of the lack of sheep! A few minutes later two more figures also appear, dogs herding the sheep with plenty of shouting and hollering. My twinge of nervousness eases, then evaporates. While the dogs run around like crazy, mountain rescue Bob and I laughed about life, relationships, house renovations and a mutual friend of ours. I'm honestly in the perfect place, having a super conversation, great company, while watching a happy Twatterdale run and explore. The light goes from sunset to gloaming, that delightful moment before dark hits and the end of the day is truly upon us. With an empty wine bottle, drop in temperatures and the wind picking up, it is time for my friend to head off back down the Fell to the safety and comfort of his own bed. His parting words are for me to stay off his mountain patch and be someone else's rescue problem. The perfect comment to end on.

After one last wee I climbed back into my tent, zip up and settled into my sleeping bag. I have got cold, which is never good on the Fells. It always takes the Twatterdale a few minutes to settle, 15 minutes on this occasion. Eventually she realised that being in the sleeping bag with me was better than sleeping on the cold floor of the tent. In she wriggles, right down to the bottom of my sleeping bag, I won't lie, I'm really relieved since my legs and feet are so cold. My living hot water bottle does the trick and in no time at all we both fall asleep. I wake-up briefly during the night, the wind is picking up and rain is falling. After an adjustment I get comfortable again, the soothing sounds of the weather lulls me back to sleep. The next time I open my eyes it is light, bright and I have a dog popping her happy face into mine. I check my phone to see what time it is, 7:25am, fabulous! Time to have coffee and explore before other people hit the fells.

With my usual coffee and caramel wafer consumed I decide to head up to the summit of Pike O'Blisco, a delightful fell which I have never quite managed to get to the top of before, for no other reason than conflicting agendas. From where I have camped it is a quick walk up and will make for some great scrambling for those who are inclined. After a couple of false summits I arrive at the top, it is so worth the morning effort. The views were stunning, even in the morning haze it really is a treat. Being on a Fell when the rest of the world is still waking up and making decisions about the day head is one of my most favourite mountain moments. You feel like you have the playground all to yourself. After a good 15 minutes of taking in the panoramic views I decide that breakfast is calling and so is that second cup of coffee! The Twatterdale and I make our way back down to our basecamp, brew up and fill our boots with food. I haven't realised just quite how hungry I am until the sausage sandwich hits my lips. The same applies to the dog, who shares sausages with me, equally as enthused.

I wash the pots in the stream, squatting down, feeling the cool water run between my fingers, I clean my teeth there too and make the decision to pack up and make my way back to the car. The sun is shining but there are dark clouds on the horizon. I don't want to leave, it's like I have claimed a patch of land as mine, even if it was just for the night, I'm not ready to give it up just yet. I pack my bag and set off back to the car, soaking up every drop of the beautiful landscape before reality sets back in. Back at the car I ease the backpack into the boot and feel the instant release in my shoulders. I feel torn between heading a bit further down the valley to find a hidden swimming spot or going home, having a nap, doing the weekly shop, knowing I will have all of Sunday to play with. I chose the latter. With the weather looking unfavourable I figure this is the sensible option. It pains me though.

The drive home is uneventful, rain showers and slow drivers test my patience but before I know it, I'm home, unlocking the door to my little slice of heaven. I dump my kit, have a much-needed shower and fall into bed. In the space of 24 hours I've had a perfect micro adventure. There are so many men and women who delay doing such things because they don't want to go alone and wait for someone else to say 'yes' to the adventure. I have hit this point in my life where I realise that I don't need a plus one to fulfil my soul. Don't get me wrong, sharing the experience with someone is beautiful, however, putting off having an experience because you are waiting to share is time lost. Seize the moment. Live now.

The connection to my resentment, that feeling deep within my gut, down in the core of my soul must be explored, although there are moments when I feel the fear of going there, because if I do it means true acknowledgement. All around me I observe a disconnect to the world, the beauty that envelops us. I watch as children in pushchairs are handed a mobile phone to keep them quiet with mind numbing cheap entertainment. I see slightly older children, all under 10 years of age throw tantrums because they have no digital access and have the inability to use their imagination to create a world of fantasy. In cafés and restaurants there are couples hunched over, nursing cups of lukewarm coffee, not making eye contact or conversing, instead they are focused on the small device held in their hands, Scrolling, scrolling and scrolling. I want to scream.

I look at the world, the people around me, family, friends, strangers, colleagues and neighbours and see stress, sickness, anxiety, exhaustion, burnout, working just to experience a two-week holiday once a year or dragging themselves through to the next weekend. We've become slaves to money, to work, to possessions, holidays, clothes, how our houses look and I fall into all of this. I'm not excluded! In theory the world has more access to 'well-being' than ever and yet obesity, cancer, and overall illness like those mentioned above are at an all-time high. We are killing ourselves with the way we live, our diets, lifestyle and stress. When will it stop? I'm sitting here in bed with my Buddha belly poking out from under my t-shirt. I ate so much last night (comfort eating) that I went to bed feeling sick. I'm aware of this, I'm aware that we move less, eat more, laugh less, connect to people less and love with imposed limits. Communities are dying, people have become so self-absorbed, no one has time for anyone anymore and segregation due to Covid is hitting hard. It is this, all of this that has made me question my existence, my purpose, the way I chose to live my life and whether it feels rich. Am I thriving or just surviving? What do I want to do with this one wild and precious life?

The industrial revolution brought so much so fast and with it our natural biorhythms were changed overnight. Gone were the days of working with natural daylight hours and the seasons. Traditional farming methods were cast aside for 'new and improved' ways of rapidly producing food and goods, which over the years has seen the introduction of chemicals and now lab grown meat. Instead of working the land, connecting to the soil and all the wonders of biodiversity, we are hunched over laptops and sat in front of computer screens for hours at a time. Once over communities would work this majestic landscape together, share and trade crops and barter hand-crafted goods, now we are encased in glass buildings with climate controlled air, false light and flickering screens. Conversation is limited, even monitored in some work places and when conversation does take place is it about the latest episode of whatever empty boxset or season of celebrity reality show that halts family time and dulls the creative mind.

The increasing and alarming number of people on medication that numbs the soul and natural emotions to deal with anxiety and depression is rising at an alarming rate. Instead of looking at the underpinning causes of the epidemic, prescriptions are handed out like sweets and the desperate recipients take them without question, because how can we question when we are kept so busy? I look at my own life, the daily cycle of rising early to walk the Twatterdale and snatch time in the fields before logging on to a day of meetings, egos and voices that want to be heard, reports and actions that are then written, often unfulfilled because there simply aren't enough hours in the day. The emails that fly around at 11pm and the need for people to be present at all hours just to prove their professional worth sickens me. Creative time is non-existent and with each passing precious moment we lose a little bit more of ourselves to the corporate machine. When did we become so consumer obsessed and strive to want more when we already have too much?

We have gone from being individuals, citizens and close knit communities to consumers, targeted by multibillion pound companies that use every opportunity to weave their marketing strategies into our crumbling world, and yet we continue to buy the lies. Media presents us with an image of wealth and ideology that simply isn't true. You scratch the surface and see that poverty, food banks, homelessness, drugs addiction, alcoholism and broken homes filled with disfunction and violence are the result of the carefully crafted marketing that is there 24 hours a day. This is not the life I want to live, this is not the tribe I belong to, this is not my heartbeat.

It's time to face the truth and give my niggle a voice. This statement alone can fill me with that sense of unease. This past Friday night I took myself off for a wild camp, not to head to the hills for my usual walking and being feral, this time it was to lean into a cold hard niggle that has been brewing for months. It started with 'what if', which as we all know could lead absolutely anywhere if you let it free, allow it to escape from its box and be allowed to run riot. And let it free I did. My 'what if', the voice of the niggle when given air time sounds like this...

What if I sold the house? What if I rented the house as a holiday let? What if I lived in a van and had a nomadic existence? What if I quit my job, and ego driven colleagues and gave that notice period? What if I get my coaching and mentoring qualification and work virtually as a self-employed coach? What if I seek out a community that is connected to the earth, a more natural way of living and being? What lies beyond the walls I have created for myself, because I too have fallen into the consumer trap of thinking I need all this 'stuff', none of which truly feeds my soul. What if my children give me the green light to do this? They are after all the only opinions that really matter to me. And so my 'what if's' have been let loose, out of the bag, running wild and free like crazy people. I've acknowledged it out loud now, it's there, it's a *thing* and I can't put it back in the box.

I know my situation isn't exceptional by any means, I work 8.30am – 5pm five days a week. I've been in my job since April 2020, working from home the whole time, bar the odd occasion where I have had a day trip out into the office. Let's go deeper, I have found what I really like doing and what my calling is while in this role, this is a gift in my view and one that I have gratitude for. It would seem I have a natural aptitude for writing leadership material, coaching, mentoring and facilitating. I love watching people hold a space of self-reflection, even if it is just for a small amount of time. Me connecting with this skill has led me to enrolling on a coaching and mentoring level five qualification. The plan started to form in my head at this point.

I sat in the gypsy wagon the other night, looking out across the fields, uninterrupted views, wildlife all around me and realised that I have everything I need and could possibly want so what is the problem? The problem is I feel the way I live is not purposeful, I'm working to pay bills, a mortgage, to eat, to head to the Lakes on a weekend in order to keep my sanity and for what? It's all to maintain the consumerism that I've created for myself. I did this, nobody else, it was 100% me! Yes, I have a home that most people would die for, it's been hard graft, it's been expensive and I have no savings. The money I earn has all gone into the fabric of my home. I have gone into the fabric of my home, it reflects me, I'm in the carefully selected books, cushions and lampshades that surround me in my false sense of security. So is it time for change? Is it time for me to truly follow my heart and explore living an alternative life? I'm holding these thoughts so carefully, they seem so fragile now they have been given power. I can't break them, I need to hold and nurture them so I can see what develops.

For years I've wanted dreadlocks but work, professionalism and judgement of others has put me off. I now have 8 tiny dreads sitting under my hair, with more being added week on week. My nose ring has made a re-appearance and my arm will have more tattoos added in October. This is me. I now want to connect to the next part of me, the 'me' that has been loitering in the background for years, too worried to fully jump out because of what others might think. This untamed soul who is filled with self- doubt, and pre-conditioned like the rest of society to find the man, get the job, have the house. But here is the thing, I want to shout 'FUCK ALL OF THAT' because it is not how I want to live, I feel suffocated by societal norms.

I have options to explore and as true to exploring all viable routes I narrow them down to this:

Option A – I sell the cottage and all the contents, everything goes, 26 years of collecting and accumulating is gone. I take the equity, buy a van, work self-employed and travel. The Risk naturally is that I might hate it and then have no home to come back to, no job, no roots, no nothing. But isn't that the point? Have less, leave the possessions and all that comes with the chattel ties and step into a more liberating space.

Option B: I rent the cottage as a holiday let for X number of weeks a year. I derive an income from this, live in a van when the cottage is let and use it as a base when not. I could also consult and work as a coach to supplement my income. I could actually save money, still travel, still have the best of both worlds so to speak. This is the less risky option, the one where I straddle both worlds. I guess the challenge there is, will I ever be free if I have one foot in the 'real world'?

And so it begins, my next step of exploration. Tomorrow I get the cottage surveyed to see roughly what it might be worth, this step alone is a heel biting reality. On Friday I have a holiday letting company coming over to again see how much/if the cottage is fit to let. It's my starting point. My financial reality check is hours away and with each hand of the ticking clock my dreams become slightly more real. I firmly believe that life presents things when the moment is right, I need to make sure I'm in a space where I'm open to hearing and feeling the change which is being offered. This will require patience; it will require planning and the support of my boys. It will pull on my fears of those negative 'what if's' and my bravery will have to be up front and central. I begin to wonder if I could trade my Fiat 500 in for a van now, rent out the cottage and live in the van locally on the weeks the cottage is let. Hold onto my full-time job and grab the extra income while possible. The thing is all of this is possible... every last scrap is possible, options A-Z are possible. The biggest decider is my boys. I need to be here for them. The Cub more than the Child but I still need to be present, to be a parent, guide and love them.

Head. Heart. Heart. Head. The cottage has been valued and I've had to think about my 'what ifs' once again. What is the right thing to do? I'm suddenly filled with the enormity of what could be life changing decisions. I take Tuesday off work and Mother Goose with my Gosling sister come over to offer moral support. I supply lunch and create a space for me to let my thoughts run riot. We sit at the bottom of the garden by the gypsy wagon, sun warming our faces and I begin to share my considerations for selling. The

Buddleia is in bloom, butterflies and bees hum all arounds us and I carefully watch this hive of activity along with the shock on the faces of my family. I sense that neither of them will tell me 'what to do' but I also sense that while they sit there in this idyllic location, they too think I'm having a midlife crisis! What is clear from them both is that they will be supportive irrespective of my final decision. Mother Goose defaults back to her standards statement, 'well, only you know what's right love'. My sister echoes this sentiment. They leave and I speculate what their conversation will cover when they are back to the confines of my sister's car.

I know deep down being a Mother Goose myself, that I absolutely need to wait until my boys are older before buggering off and doing my feral living. That van life is too much of a jump at this time and somewhere in my quest for living is a sweet spot that will fit all of us. This past week has been difficult. I've felt frustrated at the world we live in and the way we are conditioned from birth to buy into this bonkers way of being, but for now I will nurture my boys, embrace every day, grow my dreadlocks and explore this beautiful landscape that is the gift for my feet to kiss. What I can do is continue to make changes, small changes in my life that will make a big difference, this and head back up to the place that fills my soul... Wasdale.

*

The weather has been reaching higher temperatures this week, the kind of heat that leaves sweat trickling down your back and a film of dampness that covers your whole body. My hair curls, my skin glows and the dog sleeps. As the weekend approaches the camping kit comes out of the cupboard and onto the window seat. The dog stirs. By 4.45pm the car is packed and we are heading up to the place where my heart sings louder than ever… Wasdale. It's 90 miles away and sits at the far western side of the Lake District. The drive over is challenging, only because the Twatterdale is struggling in the heat, something which I've not experienced with her before. This surprised me if honest and what should have been a 2.5-hour journey turned into 3 hours with the occasional start and stop on route. Before we had even travelled 10 miles she had an accident on the back seat of the car. A first for her, the distressed look in her eyes alone told me that she was so terribly sorry. We cuddle before setting off again.

The road narrows, the trees on either side block the view of the surrounding fells, but I still get the sense they are ever present. I drive over the cattle grid and know that within a second the most breath-taking view is going to reveal itself. It never disappoints, ever! I have to stop the car and take a moment to absorb the majestic fells, the scree dropping down into the lake, the late day sun turning Yewbarrow, Great Gable and Lingmel a delightful russet. These are the highest of fells and the deepest lake and here I am, about to embrace and connect to all of what this majestic land has to offer. I could explode. I'm that happy.

I drive down the side of the lake on the single-track road and find somewhere to leave the car for a couple of days. The Twatterdale is now beside herself with excitement. I quickly change into my hiking boots and load the 45lb backpack onto my back, grab the dog and off we go. We navigate bracken that is waist high, checking the map every so often to give me the reassurance I'm heading in the right direction. Before long the lake is left behind and a series of stunning waterfalls are next to me, guiding me to the tarn where I will spend the night. The light is changing, it becomes mellow and the heat dips, becoming a warmth rather than searing. I cross the stream, continue to climb leaving the path behind in my effort to search for the tarn. The Twatterdale dips in and out of bracken, while I can't see her, the movement of the plant gives away her hiding place.

After 2 hours and 10 minutes of assent my home for the night is in view. It is as majestic as I have imagined and so worth the effort to get there. I spot one other tent, pitched discreetly away from the water's edge. I wander for a further 10 minutes looking for the perfect spot to pitch up. I ease the backpack off my aching shoulders and stretch my body out, reaching out for the moon with my arms which is smiling back down at me in all her summer glory. It's starting to get dark now, I have a small window to set up camp and eat. Once settled I sit there and marvel at the moon, which offers up a lovely bit of light, no need for a head torch, the surrounding sky is a strange shade of dark blue, then fading into light blue with the surrounding fells forming a black backdrop. I am so bloody happy. The temperature drops but not to a level of discomfort. I'm tired, I climb into my tent, get into my sleeping bag but can't quite manage to fall asleep. I know why, it's the sky you see. I know that on a night like this the stars will put on the show of a lifetime and my need to see this is more powerful than sleep. I drift off and then at some early hour I wake just enough to unzip the tent and stick my head out. The beauty is beyond words, beyond a picture, it is collateral, overwhelming and mine to hold. The absence of light pollution means that the true magnitude of space is shown at its very best, the Milky Way is just visible, I want to capture it but I can't, only in my memory will the image exist. Now I can sleep. Now I'm ready.

I sleep one of those amazing deep sleeps and wake the next morning to the wriggling of the dog, who is itching to go out and explore. I unzip the tent and feel the cool morning air hit my skin. I walk barefoot down to the tarn, boil water and drink my fresh coffee while the sun rises and the promise of a super-hot day begins. After my coffee I strip off and go for a dip in the tarn, what a morning treat this is! After I dry off and eat breakfast it is time to decamp and head off for a day of adventure, with the dog at my heels we head up even higher.

We hit the summit of Red Pike and then head over to Scoat Fell. The rocks are hard to navigate with my backpack on, my centre of gravity is off and this always makes me slow my pace. Higher we climbed and before long Steeple is in sight. I decided to hide my backpack and tackle Steeple with physical freedom. It doesn't disappoint, the views are too much for my eyes to process, I take my time and soaked it all up while my dog seeks refuge in the shade. I head back towards Scoat Fell and decide Pillar is next on the list. This is where it all gets a bit tricky. For starters the heat is hitting both of us and my usually bouncy dog is showing signs of exhaustion. I'm worried but know that given my grid reference there is no option but to keep going until I can navigate off the fells.

I have underestimated the challenge of Wind Gap, a challenge I normally would take in my stride but not with 45lbs strapped to me. I began the assent. The midday heat is a killer and my pace is slow now. The dog is struggling to find routes over the rocks and the risk of me lifting her while maintaining my balance is becoming a worry. I reached for a rock, I go to pull myself up but the rock is loose. Before I know what was happening the boulder has moved past me and is picking up speed while heading towards a man who is around 10ft below me. I fall flat on my stomach, gather my senses so I can react and shout for the man below to move. He does so quickly, with the rock missing him by only a few inches. I needed to get off this patch and regain my composure. I'm shaken, dehydrated and concerned about Miss Twattypants.

The arrival of Pillar summit is a relief, but not for the dog. There is no shade, nowhere to recover, just more heat. I choose not to dwell, instead we made our way down to Black Sail Pass where I know waterfalls will welcome us. The descent is challenging, more rocks to navigate, more scree to slide on. Just before I reached Black Sail Pass, I meet a delightful man called Tim. He works as a Chemist at the powerplant. We sit on a rock and chat like old friends. He is in his 20's and me in my 40's, both navigating the dating world. For 30 minutes we exchange our stories, bond over our desire for love and companionship. After a wonderful conversation we part ways. The people I've met on the Fells never disappoint, if only everyone were like this daily, in normal day to day life.

I head down the Pass, hungry, hot, tired and knowing that a second night on the Fells is out of the question. The waterfall is in sight, but before that and before I know what is happening, I fall over, slipping without control on the scree, my leg bending at a painful angle. I sit there for a minute and take my time in regaining my composure while carefully moving my leg back into a normal position. The warning shots of life have been fired off and I need to call it a day. We stop at the waterfall and cool off, I slide my boots, then socks off and dangle my feet in the cool water. We both sit. The dog pants, then immerses herself in the water to cool her stomach. I want to do the same but decide against it. After a substantial rest the Wasdale Head Inn is in sight, 45 minutes and I know we will be there. We walk into the cool of the pub, it is quiet, empty almost. I ease myself into my favourite booth and sigh with relief. The pint I drink is worth the wait and my decision to call it a day is most certainly the right one. I chat with the waitress who is a dreadlocked goddess, her face is splattered with freckles, she has long toned limbs, a pierced septum and an air of wild beauty. She offers to drive me to my car so that the Twatterdale's paws don't blister on the tarmac, I'm so grateful. We chat and I feet delight in the shadow of this free-spirited creature. We part ways and off I drive, home, shower, bed, rest. I feel full. Whole. I'm so happy. I also think I've reached a decision.

*

The feeling of needing to sell my 'little slice of heaven' and make a change in how I live hasn't lifted or shifted, it's just got stronger. I feel like someone is tapping me on my shoulder, or between my shoulder blades, pushing me to move forward and trust my instinct, that this is the right thing to do. I *know* it is the right thing to do. There are so many reasons that are tangible and then there are also feelings that I can't label or hold, it's just instinct, deep and primal. I've delved deeper into what my gut feeling is telling me; what is it I'm seeing, hearing, sensing and experiencing that propels me to make this change?

I know that 9-5 grind is done for me, I know that the way things are shifting with Covid and people being segregated, told if they don't vaccinate that they won't be able to go out, into bars, restaurants and from what I heard yesterday in a meeting – work! I don't want to be a slave to a mortgage, irrespective of how beautiful the cottage is. I feel weighed down by the sheer responsibility of the house, belongings and duty to work 40 hours a week just to live. But it's not really living, is it? Is it thriving or surviving? I feel I lose a little part of me as time goes by, but yet find new deeper inner parts of me that are wanting to come to the surface and leap out. My time is now. I know my time is now.

I continue to go into places in my mind and explore the 'what ifs', the fears, the dreams and have settled somewhere that feels so damn right. As much as I desire to buy a van and live a more nomadic existence, I also know that the Man-Cub and Man-Child still need their momma. It is with this in mind that I settled on buying a narrowboat. The network locally is the Leeds to Liverpool canal and I figure I can float around in that vicinity, live a freer life and be closer to the baddies. The question now is, how do I make this happen?

The cottage has been valued, I now know what I have to play with for cash, I've also been looking at boats both online and physical viewings. I've found a 'floating slice of heaven' that I keep going back to. She's a more mature vessel, small, traditional and a real delight when it comes to potential. I've viewed her twice and know that this is where my heart is settling. I also know nothing about boats, or life on the canal. But what I do know is that I will learn, I will find a way of taking this leap of faith and stepping into a space which will take me onto the next stage of this life journey. Letting go of a cottage full of contents has been something which I've had to get my head around. That point where I look at all my possessions and know that each and every one of them will be let go of. I feel some are tied to me with invisible string, I look around me and ponder what small items will remain knotted

and, which lengths of string I will let go of.   What
matters? Does any of it matter? A beautiful friend of
mine once said "there are no pockets in a shroud". Hold
that though and give it the attention it deserves.

The last two weeks has seen a shift in my heart,
my mindset has experienced a dramatic landslide. I
have mentally started to let go and move into a new
more liberating space in my head. I am also the new
owner of 'a little slice of floating heaven'. What has
been humbling is that my Dad and a friend have helped
me short term financially to make this dream a reality.
My cottage just needs to sell so I can move into the boat
full time. I wait for the *For Sale* sign to go up. I don't
know how I will feel when this moment happens. The
belief that people have in me doing this has warmed my
heart, made me cry and treasure that love and kindness
is there in abundance. I've also had people state that
"you are having a crisis, this is nothing but a mid-life
crisis". This statement hurt and it has come from a
couple of close friends, all with good intentions. I see it
this way, perhaps it is a mid-life awakening and not a
crisis. Half empty or half full glass?

The day is here. Today is the day I take my
floating slice of heaven out on the canal. I'm nervous.
Excited. And have no bloody clue what I'm doing! I wish
more people would embrace their dreams, hold their

fears and step into the unknown. Heart full. Belly empty. The day awaits. How hard can it be?

*

The *For Sale* sign is now outside my cottage for all to see. The questions from the neighbours begin immediately, which is natural. I give the estate agents permission and a final nod that the property video and pictures can go live on their website and on Rightmove. I have no idea what to expect, I just know that this is so very real all of a sudden. The next morning I receive a call of the agent to tell me they have 8 viewings booked for Saturday morning, 3 booked for Friday and I decide that now is a good time to head to the hills. I don't know what it is that has suddenly unsettled me but I know I can't be here when strangers walk around my home. I just can't. This time, instead of a solo camp I drag the Man-cub with me so that he too can have time to digest the reality of this situation.

The Man-Cub has new kit to test and so it is on the last sunny Friday in the summer holidays, we head to the hills of the Lake District to see what is on offer, likely for the last time this season. Picking a route which wasn't going to be too difficult was my task, but also picking something which would offer up a variety of landscapes and experiences too. I settle on Thirlmere, a delightful valley, which is tree-lined and often overlooked, it's also an area which I have neglected to explore. We parked up on the westside of the reservoir and I immediately fall in love with the area and the fact that hardly anyone seems to use this road. I refuse to pay for parking when the money goes to feeding yet more greedy companies, so the task was 'where does Mumma dump the car?' Max is clearly more sensible than me and applied lots of logic to the mix, where I would have just plonked it anywhere in the hope that it was still there the next day. As luck would have it, we found a place with our name on it and I tucked the car neatly in, we grab our backpacks and the dog and off we go.

The First mile takes us on a footpath at the edge of the lake. It was stunning. There are waterfalls feeding the lake (technically a reservoir), which the Cub absolutely loves. While most teenagers don't normally express their joy, I know mine was happy due to the number of photos he is taking. I marvelled at the amount of signs saying, 'no camping', 'no parking', 'no fires', 'no litter', 'no swimming'. It is this that feeds my frustration, but for now let's leave that one be. The water level is low, making the islands in what should be the middle of the lake accessible... the temptation to camp on one of the islands was almost too much... almost.

We reach Armboth, which means that it is time to start climbing out of the valley and over to the next valley where our first destination calls us. The climb out is tree-lined and the waterfalls make a musical backdrop to our chatter. And chatter we do. The Cub tells me about his trip to Birmingham and how it was a far cry from this. How amazed he is that in one day you can experience so much variety and how lucky we are to live where we do. He's 15 and gets it. I want to celebrate the moment but also needed to remain cool. The Cub had braces fit the previous week and eating was proving a problem. We stop for a snack, perched on a rock, high above the trees and while I devoured my sandwich, the Cub nibbles on his. The vista is breath-taking.

Before long the trees are behind us and we find ourselves on exposed moorland. After all the heavy rain it becomes clear that the main challenge now is keeping our feet dry. This is one epic fail and we give into nature and very soggy boots. We reached the top of the fell in no time at all, where we are met with one hell of a panoramic view. The Cub sits on a cairn and soaks it all up. I know that in the next 15 minutes Watendlath would be in sight. My Grandad loved this place, I have never been and for some reason when I woke up this morning it was that name planted in my head. A gift from Grandad I believe. After a short rest we set off walking down the fell into the next valley and the idyllic view of Watendlath is upon us. I now get why Grandad loved this place.

Even the Cub is taken back by this fairy-tale spot and at 5pm there are no visitors to be found which suited both of us just fine. We sit on the iconic bridge and eat chocolate while the Twatterdale runs around like crazy. I look at the map and gently announce that we needed to climb back out of the valley (it was seriously steep) to find the path that would take us to Blea Tarn. I half expected a bit of a strop off the Cub but he was absolutely fine and said that the view down to the hamlet was so beautiful that the climb back out really was no bother. And so off we went. Once we reached the path, we quickly made headway, after crossing the second stream we found the most majestic patch that screamed so loudly "camp here, camp here". The view was so breath-taking that we both paused to consider our options. It is once again the Cub who insists we carry on to Blea Tarn so that we don't have as far to walk the next day. I also know that the weather was due to change and his point is spot on! But I still found it hard to tear myself away from this perfect pitch. I circle it on the map for next time.

We continued to walk across quite desolate fells and more to the point, endless bogs. We are soaked and hungry, I also know the Cub is getting tired now. Luckily the tarn appeared and the discussion of where to camp for the night is suddenly on the table. We both have our eye on a particular spot but unfortunately the crossing of a stream, which flows out of the tarn was too difficult to cross. I suggest we continue to head up the fell and camp above the tarn, grabbing the last bit of sun for the day in the process. The Cub is not happy, but with some coaxing and encouragement we found a patch that offered up a pretty spectacular view.

I have two tents to pitch, which is no problem. I also have a very excited teenager who is about to get into his own tent, which he later said, "is the first home of my own", this makes my heart sing. While the cub sorts his nest out, I set to work pitching my own tent, while the Twatterdale continues to run around like a nutter. Next is dinner, a task which is going to be testing since water is limited and due to the bogs, we have not camped near a source. I manage and the Cub has a full tummy in no time. I then feed myself and climb into my sleeping bag. The sun had set and the sky is a riot of colours, ambers, russets and soft gold. In our respective tents we chat about the view and the fact I have a dog who still doesn't want to come to bed. Finally it is time to zip up and snuggle down, a task which can't take place until a certain dog is caught and dragged into the tent!

I don't have the best night's sleep due to being on a slight slope, I find myself sliding to one end of the tent with a dog doing exactly the same. I do manage to get about 6 hours, which suits me fine. The next day is a total contrast to the previous evening, with visibility so low that we can't even see the tarn that glistened so beautifully the night before. This amuses the Cub no end and gives me the nudge to move on with making coffee. I know the weather is coming in thick and fast and that getting off the fell is our primary goal. We packed up, put on soaking wet socks and boots, agree breakfast will wait and headed off down into the Thirlmere valley one again.

Before long we were met with trees and woodland. The path this time takes us directly through the woodland, which for both of us is a delight. We look at new potential places to camp if we come up here again, we enjoy the sound of the birds and waterfalls, which guide us down to the valley bottom. We find a tarn, which has a healthy coating of lily pads covering the surface, some already in bloom. I also realise that I need a different OS map if I am to navigate us back to the car, the map I need is on the coffee table at home. Guess work from here on in!

We have a couple of false starts, but perhaps this was a serendipitous moment? We wander through waist high ferns and find ourselves on the top of a spectacular viewing point. We both take a moment to soak in our surroundings and then the Cub states that he recognises the waterfall on the other side of the lake and that we are nowhere near the car! After a quick discussion we decided the best and most sensible thing to do was head back to the small tarn we had passed and look for a logical path that would take us to the valley. We found the path and before long were back in the trees, working our way down at quite a pace.

And just like that, we find the road. The next task is to find the car! We walk about a mile and a half until my little red fiat pops into view. The Cub is relieved and plonks himself in the passenger seat, whips off his shoes and socks, then chomps on more chocolate. With the Twatterdale in the back seat already snoozing, it's time to drive home. In the space of 24 hours we experience two stunning valleys, chatted about anything and everything and became at one with nature. I'm tired. Happy. Proud. We both agreed that next time the Man-Child needs to come with us for a complete family outing. But until then we will stick with movie nights and pizza.

It's amazing what happens when you decide to sell your house and contents, people suddenly descend, which quite frankly is amazing! I've had two of my close friends come and earmark furniture which they want to take. I also wait patiently for the arrival of my dad, who

I've not seen in over two years now. The cottage sold within 24 hours, exciting but daunting, the wheels really now are in motion. I just hope the sale goes through okay and that I can make this transition onto the boat asap. But in the meantime I spend time flitting between the boat and the cottage, most of my attention is on the boat though, with sanding down wood, taking up carpet tiles and laminate flooring being my task.

The boat now resembles a scruffy dust ball and the Man-Child looks like an orange Oompa Loompa from Willy Wonker and the Chocolate Factory, after sanding 30 years of oil and stain off the wood. Still, even if the boat is a mess, it won't stop me taking my family out for a cruise up and down the canal this coming weekend. I just need to remember how to steer her, turn her on and off and tie knots. My Dad arrives Friday lunchtime, I take half a day off work so we can spend time together. It's great to see him, perm and all! Serious to God he's got a bloody perm! This weekend is going to be a big weekend for me. For the first time in my life I will be with both parents, 46 and only now is this happening. I've never been in the same space with them, together at the same time. It's a strange sensation and I suddenly feel like I'm a child again. There is a plan for the weekend, Saturday we take the boat out and then in the evening go for a curry. But first I need to feed the Man-Child, Man-Cub and my Dad.

My dad and his curls are on form and so are the boys, the conversation flows with ease, everyone is laughing and the tears roll down my face with the hilarious conversation going on around me. By 10pm I'm ready for bed, I genuinely have had the best night, it's amazing how the conversation can turn to sex at the drop of a hat, not helped by my Dad and the Man-Child. The sense of humour this family has is second to none!

I wake up the next morning to find my dad plonked downstairs already tucking in to his hundredth cup of tea. I forget how much tea he drinks! We have a slow start; I message my Mum and give the orders of when and where to meet up. I arrive at the boat to find the boys already aboard. The Man-Cub is sitting on the roof and the Man-child is dressed as Captain Jack Sparrow! The laughter starts immediately. I ease my mum and her husband out of the car. Mum's husband had a stroke last year and is now somewhat disabled. The comedy act begins! It's like a geriatric's day out. Easing my Mum, Dad and Mum's husband on the boat was nothing short of hilarious. Dad falls over at the best of times due to the impact of chemo, Mick (Mum's husband) struggles to walk quarter of a mile and has very little balance and my Mum is daft as a brush. The Man-Child helps the geriatrics onto the boat and I have the task of taking her down the canal, turning her around and heading into Skipton.

The Man-Cub is on the roof looking cool and having an amazing time, the Man-Child hanging onto the sides and my Dad wondering where the cups of tea are. I'm a bag of nerves and don't feel I have a handle on this situation at all. I manage to turn the boat around and head back towards Skipton, this alone was a new task and one which I knew I needed to master quickly. On the way into town I see a familiar figure walking down the canal, it's the boy's other Grandma, who declares from the towpath that I am completely nuts. After mooring up for 10 minutes, more conversations are had by all and I find myself rounding up old people before we can finally set off (again) to Skipton, the phrase "herding cats" comes to mind. The aim of the task is to get the boat into the canal basin, reverse her up for fuel and water and then set back off. I manage through sheer luck to reverse her and moor up, I can feel the colour in my cheeks through embarrassment, it would seem moving a boat is a spectator sport! As soon as the ropes are tied the men folk are off the boat and straight into the pub. Dad and Mum guzzle cups of tea, the rest were on pints.

Once the tank is filled and bill settled we set back off again, I quickly realise I've forgotten the Twatterdale, who is still at the pub. Much to everyone's amusement I managed to make ground and get close enough to the bank for her to jump back on board. I feel exhausted already, as we head back out of Skipton, the theme tune to Pirates of the Caribbean is playing at full volume thanks to the Man-Child. Today is quite frankly one of the most hilarious afternoons I've had in a long time. It is chaos in a bottle.

In the evening we head out for a curry, it is a lovely, relaxed evening but nothing tops off the day that we all had just experienced. Sunday rolls round with a secret speed and before long I'm saying goodbye to my Dad and heading up to bed. It really has been a fabulous few days, but boy am I tired. My Dad never stops talking and I really am not used to being around people anymore. I need to think about how I integrate myself back into humanity!

It's been a busy time and making the life changing decision to sell the cottage has caught up with me both physically and emotionally. I feel like I'm straddling two worlds, one which I live in now, comfort, water, appliances and one where I'm heading, which is pure off grid living. The boat is coming along nicely, the more I do the more I get to know her, I feel like I'm slowly undressing her, checking out her curves and finding the most bizarre wiring set up possible. I took pleasure in taking down the curtains, which most certainly were a classic 1990 style, stripping back the wood, taking up the floors and getting rid of the awful chemical smelling cassette toilet have all been the focus for the past few weeks. I tend to finish work at 5pm from the cottage and then head straight down to the boat for more DIY antics. What this evening ritual has made me realise is that we are heading into autumn. From the start of September daylight was still plentiful until 8.30pm, even later. And now as the month has progressed, I am done by 7pm at the very latest. The leaves are changing colour and the temperature is starting to vary. I have to move the boat every 14 days, which works wonderfully since I have the Man-Cub and it would seem he enjoys the experience of going up and down the canal.

My little slice of floating heaven is starting to morph into what will be home. The gas-powered fridge went to the tip, the cassette toilet joined it and I now have one bucket to wee in and another to poo in. The poo bucket will be managed as a compost toilet, something my family haven't yet got their head around. The Cub in particular is on lockdown with this concept and says there is no way he will ever use the toilet on the boat. It shows how far removed we have become from basic nature and how conditioned we are to convenience. I on the other hand am looking forward to being at one with nature, moving every 14 days and having to be more resourceful. This is the start of off grid living.

Taking the floors up was the job from hell. There was this delightful combo of laminate, carpet tiles and actual carpet, some of which was stuck to the walls for insulation. It took the best part of a week to remove the floors, a job that I never want to have to do again! The dust and muck was something else and working in a small space was interesting at best. Interesting yet comfortable, because it is my new space. The bathroom has slowly started to be transformed and my excitement has grows with each daily visit. I know that a year from now it will be all bedded in, home from home and a true floating nest. Evening trips to the pub have become a frequent occurrence and exercise has become extinct. Both the twatterdale and I are getting chunkier by the week and I have simply vowed to not get my knickers in a twist about this, I figure once this crazy transition period is over life will settle back down again. But for now I flit between my two worlds and wonder what life will be like when I have no bricks and mortar? My little slice of floating heaven is looking amazing, light and airy, which is in complete contrast to my cottage. I feel lighter on her, especially when the sun shines through the windows and the reflection of the water plays across the ceiling. The whole place glows with love and I glow too. One of the things I delight in is watching my beloved dog sit on the side of the canal, with every passer-by stopping to stroke her, belly rubs resume without shame! She has taken to what will be this new life of mine, soon I will do the same.

I've just had this past week off work, it's been a blend of dreadlocks, packing, renovating, feeling anxious, feeling frustrated and feeling like part of me has drifted somehow. With this epic change in life comes another change in life, which is tapping me on the shoulder. I'm in the perimenopausal phase where hot sweats, especially at night are becoming frequent, anxiety has increased, my mood is a bit erratic at times and my tolerance for idiots is far less than normal. I'm also looking at my own body with wonder since it's starting to look and feel different. I'm mindful that since the beginning of August my diet and exercise habits have gone and the pub with a frequency of takeaways has crept in, a habit I've never had before. I've always cooked and planned for the week ahead but suddenly I find myself eating nothing but crap and the wine intake has most certainly increased. My skin is different and the lines around my eyes are deeper. I'm going to do my best to embrace this next chapter of my life, not battle it.

It's my sense of identity which has caused me the most confusion. I don't mean internally; I actually feel more certain of myself and my purpose than ever. Externally is the issue. I no longer know what to wear, my sense of style and groove has vacated and I don't know quite how or when this happened. It doesn't help that I've spent 18 months working from home and now I suddenly need to wear office clothes. How do women move through this stage in life and maintain looking and feeling amazing. The boys always advise me to wear what I love and rock it! With this in mind I have a trip to Leeds planned, new bras for me will be on the menu! Watch this space, it's a desperate one.

Already this month is escaping me. I love this time of year, the cloud inversion, the cool mornings, the appreciation I have for warmth left in the sun and the beautiful russets, golds and last drops of green hanging on in nature. Normally, I head up to the Lake District to soak up the best of what it has to offer but this year I'm still in the process of straddling two worlds. I'm trying to find my groove with it, slowly selecting items from the cottage and working through detachment. Adding them onto sale and swap sites and watching new owners come and collect 'things' which have been part of my life. My boys are also watching and the Man-Cub in particular is struggling to let go of his attachments to the things he has known for 15 years. It continues to amaze me the amount of energy we put into 'stuff' and not people.

*

My shopping trip to Leeds went ahead as planned, my search for clothes to fit my ever changing body did not, however, go to plan, instead came back with a floral velvet chair and 3 amazing mugs. I'm not sure exactly what happened but it was a successful shopping trip for my little slice of floating heaven and nothing else. The boat has been coming on a treat and with it I figure it is time to start padding it out with stuff which will make it home. I've carefully select the items, which have made the cut from the cottage to the boat, the boys too have helped in this process, which I think we have all found a bit of an emotional challenge. Either way, the daily bags for life continue to make their way down to the boat from the cottage, one place is starting to feel like home, the other a space which I once knew as home. I feel unexpected emotional conflict with every book that is boxed up, every item sold or gifted to friends. The three of us are unsettled in every way possible.

The doorway onto the boat is only 20" wide and therefore anything which goes on has to fit through that gap... which rules out all my existing furniture. I won't lie, this I found hard because we have always had a peacock blue velvet chair, a chair which we are all strangely attached to, including the Twatterdale.

Conversations that matter have taken place with one of us sat in this chair, tears, laugher and sometimes the quiet act of reading have all been woven into its fabric. During my trip to Leeds it seemed only right that when I stumbled across a replacement the purchase became one of necessity. This will also double up as my work chair, which is my justification for spending a pretty penny on this item! There are poppies on it, large, vibrant and stunning set against a backdrop of fuchsia and teal. It has its funk going on, but it will never be the same as the chair I'm about to say goodbye to.

Each night once I've returned from the boat, I take down another pair of curtains in the house and alter them to fit the boat. I can't sew for love nor money but I've given this my best shot, I think part of this task is emotional attachment and not being ready to let go. Some of the hems are at a jaunty angle but that alone makes me smile, it is after all, all part of this journey of transition. This week also brought the arrival of my new mattress. I small double size which barely fits through the bow doors. With a lot of sweating, swearing and pushing we ease the mattress in, new sheets in a pink brush cotton are added, floral pillowcases and a small reading light make this space cosy. I have curtains around the cabin bed, a built in book case at the end and fairy lights to add a layer of comfort. My new velvet chair sits proudly in the corner of my living room space, new chunky mugs hang above the oven, there is a colourful rug on the newly laid oak floor, candles provide the main source of lighting and the time has finally come for me to spend my first night on my little slice of floating heaven. I'm excited, content and feel so damn calm. I'm not sure what it is about being on the boat but I immediately feel this sense of peace wash over me, it's like someone standing behind me, gently placing their hands on my shoulders, then whispering in my ear that it is all okay. I risk lighting the fire; the flue clearly needs cleaning because the boat fills instantly with smoke. I'm unphased and before long the wood burner is pumping out a delightful heat. I sit on the bench at the bow of *my* boat, fairy lights above me, the moon reflecting on the water and there isn't a sound.

I sit, no music, no internet, no books, no company, just me, the moon and my new home. I pour a dram of whiskey, turning the crystal glass in my hand and reflect on how I've got here. It's not been easy and I've met some delightful and interesting people along the way. All teachers in one way or another. I ponder on who I might meet next, what lessons I will learn, what mark will they leave on me? How exciting to be able to assume all of these things. It makes me realise once again how much I take life for granted, that there will always be a tomorrow when the reality is we don't really know.

Autumn

A week ago today I moved onto ' My little slice of
floating Heaven', the cottage hasn't completed just yet
but I couldn't sit there any longer in what has become
the shell of my home. It has tugged at my heartstrings
too much and the Man-cub also has unravelled with the
sale of each item. I underestimated this fully and while I
know in my heart it is the right thing to do, five years of
our fingertips, footprints and love have gone into this
place. I no longer recognise it as home. I was convinced
that I would be carried out of the cottage in a box at
some crazy ripe old age, my boys were too. Yet here I
am, a week before completion and I feel I'm about to
walk out of the door for the very last time. I will
remember many of my neighbours with fondness, their
own peculiarities and that I had the privilege of
spending five years in this magical place.

Today my beautiful friend helped me load my car and
hers to take the last of my stuff to the boat, it was the
same friend who helped me load my car and move into
the cottage. I believe we both battled with emotions.
We ate toast, drank coffee and I gave her a guided tour
of my 35ft home. We also moved the boat from one
village to the outskirts of Skipton, again a joy to be had
for both of us. And so it is, I'm in. I live aboard a
beautiful 31 year old boat that is a total reflection of me

in every way possible. At the risk of sounding self-ordained, I'm also seriously proud of myself. It is a bold and brave move, one most people sit and scratch their heads at, but for me it feels right. My heart sings, my dog is content and so am I. It's the little things like having a bed with curtains that you can pull across to keep the heat in when winter is at its most ferocious. It's pink brushed cotton bedding and floral pillowcases. It's having all my favourite books stacked at the end of my bed with a content Twatterdale asleep in front of them. It's knowing that I can move to have a night under the stars away from noise and people or simply stay in town and grab beer anytime I like. I'm a snail with her home on her back, I can retreat or move.

This weekend has also given me a firm grounding that, while I am happy as a pig in shit being a snail, the Man-cub is far from not. I will be the first to admit that my stress levels are through the roof, I'm juggling a lot and that means I'm not at my best. I have no real clue what I'm doing when it comes to managing this vessel, this comes out in ways of me being short tempered, snippy and damn right rude. I've failed to recognise how much selling the cottage is impacting the Cub. He is not in a good place, has become withdrawn and very rude, tearful at times and almost like a mirror version of me at my worst. Him being on his mobile all the time while the rest of us running around moving, fixing and carrying sent me over the edge. I guess the Cub is not used to me getting angry, raising my voice and losing my shit. But lose it I did and I have regretted that moment since.

I'm not proud, what should have been a special weekend was tense, fractious, emotional and generally bloody awful. He went back to his Dad's early, which resulted in the predictable phone call from his Dad essentially telling me what a selfish and irresponsible decision moving onto a boat is. It doesn't matter how much time lapses, he still bubbles with resentment towards me and I fear that will never change, but he is an amazing father to my boys and that is what matters the most! I'm not sure I've ever fit in the box most people call *life* and I suspect my life will continue to be one of adventure, exploration and trying things which push me out of my comfort zone. I suppose what I need to hold onto is how I bring the Child and Cub on the journey in a way which is fun and empowering without causing trauma and unsettlement. Give me a manual please, I don't know how to do this and already feel I'm failing massively.

What has amazed me the most is that because I follow my dreams and ambition I'm classed as selfish and irresponsible, if it was a man doing this he would be brave, courageous and it would be totally fucking acceptable. Last night I felt sad, like a genuinely shit Mum who has let her children down, this morning I feel angry that someone has made me feel like this, or perhaps I know there is an element of truth and that I should have waited until the Cub was older? And so I continue to process... What I land on every time is how amazing women are. We are strong, resilient people who navigate so much. From *growing* a human and the pain we endure bringing that human into the world, periods, menopause, fighting for our rights and reaching beyond the centuries of the defined role we were given. But then are we trying to be and do too much? All lines have been erased, with genders, expectations and "normality" being totally re-written. It is this that causes me to pause and reflect. I am perfectly aware of my limitations, I do like it when a man or woman holds open the door for me, when manners take the centre stage not the ego. If I were to think back on my time as a woman and as a mum, I would most certainly do things differently. For starters I wouldn't have clambered the career ladder, battling for my place in the spotlight. I would have been with my children, helping them grow, being there at the school gate and not in a vortex of hurry. But for now I have to build some delicate bridges, hold some hands and nurture feelings of loss that both my boys might be feeling.

*

October is coming to an end and I've also come to the end of the first week living aboard 'my little slice of floating heaven'. It's been a funny old week with still having one foot in the world of my cottage while my heart is now on my boat, I'm almost ready to hand over those keys. At the weekend I decided to bring the boat into the centre of Skipton and enjoy the vibe that comes with a bustling town. What I hadn't quite thought about was the constant traffic past my window, people peering in, dogs cocking their leg on my ropes and the drunken revelry (not me for once) coming home from the pub. So on Sunday I decided to move her to the bottom of the park, which resulted in the Man-Cub wanting pretty much nothing to do with me because his school peers walk that way and it's simply "too humiliating". I feel my failure rate as a mum is going through the roof now and no matter what I do, it will cause offence.

Even mooring at the bottom of the park has come with some challenges. The first night a terrible storm came through and while I lay there tucked up in my cosy duvet, dog sleeping at my feet, I couldn't help but wonder how much water was coming in at the stern? Sleep. Try to sleep. It's quite hard to sleep when your house is being bashed on the side of the canal all night. It wasn't so much rocking, more being absolutely smashed about. It was a night where sleep wasn't fully on the agenda and I accepted that perhaps this could be the sign of things to come throughout winter. The next morning the weather still hadn't let up and both the Twatterdale and I reluctantly got our coats and wellies on and headed into the park. It didn't disappoint, the autumn leaves were in full glory, some clinging to the branches while others created a carpet of the finest colours for me to walk on. I felt like Royalty being welcomed by nature. We came home, dried off and I got ready to log on for more endless screen time of the 9-5pm grind. Right now I am questioning if there are yet more changes to come. I have quickly learned that my current mooring spot doesn't have the best Internet signal, video calls are a challenge because of this and my frustration grows. I still feel groggy due to the lack of sleep, the weather is refusing to give up its rage and I continued to feel utterly shite about the Man-cub. I also realised that I was running very low on coal and wood. This past week I have been making after work pilgrimages to the supermarket to buy their overpriced low quality fuel. So I made the call to a local merchant... which went like this:

        'Good morning, I wondered if I could place an order for some coal?'
'Aye'
'I live on a canal barge and wondered if you could maybe deliver'

'Aye'

'Do you also do wood and kindling'

'Aye lass, we do. Where is tha moored?'

'Near the bridge at the bottom of Aireville park'

At this point he stops talking to me and turns to his colleague to have a conversation...

'There's a lass moored at bottom of park, get loaded up lad and teck her some stuff'

'Oh thank you, will you be delivering today?'

'Aye we will at that'

'Brilliant, I really appreciate it, roughly what time?'

'Dunno, today sometime'

'Do you think it might be morning or afternoon'

'Just when he gets there love'

'Right okay. So will your driver come down to the boat?'

'No love, we don't take stuff down towpath, come t'bridge and sort thee sen out'

'Oh okay'

'Has thee a trolly?'

'Er no'

'Well, ya'll have to carry it then'

'Okay. So to confirm, 100kg of coal, 3 big bags of logs and 2 bags of kindling'

'Sounds about reet'

'How much will that be please?'

'I can't tot that up now love, me driver will tell ya'

'Do I pay him cash?'

'It's up to you lass, sort it out later, I've got work t'do'.

And so my initiation into boat life starts. A neighbouring boater loaned me his trolly. I now NEED a trolly. When the driver arrived he asked me if I wanted to take one bag at a time. I said to load two at a time. At this he looked surprised. I dragged the coal and wood to the boat and then looked at the black sooty mess which was me, dripping with water due to the relentless rain and realising that I had all of this to lift onto the roof of my boat. Fuck. Like Fuck. I was late for my meeting, I turned my camera on and the women looking back at me was covered in coal dust, hair clinging to her head and a streak of black down her cheek.

As the day wore on I continued to work, not with heart and soul but more a questioning of what it is I'm really doing. I don't mean boat life, this has been an active choice, I mean the 9-5pm. I have been doing it to try and make a difference to the lives of students and staff, but lately I'm questioning this. I see other boaters around me, their boats held together with tape and upside down buckets as caps for their flues. They make do. There is nothing flash, nothing posh, just practical. It's not about money, it's about life and satisfaction.

I asked my neighbour, whose job is to take out the day trip boats, if he actually enjoys his job? 'I love it, I'm doing what I love. I take hordes of tourists up and down the canal, turn the boat around and bring them back again, it makes me happy'. In my world of status, ego and endless meetings I do wonder how such simplicity can bring so much joy. There is contentment with this chap, no worries, no concerns, he is here, in this present moment living life on his terms. I feel a pang of envy. The roof of his boat is held together by Duct Tape, the sides look like they are made from plyboard and he has eyes that are the brightest of blue and sparkle with delight. I find myself re-evaluating yet again. I won't rush anything but I need to think what this next summer might hold. My hope, my goal was to cut my hours down, maybe even take the summer off. But how will I manage without a big wage? I've already come to the conclusion that fuel is expensive, especially when you work from home. But what if I got rid of my car? What if I got a job under £12K a year and didn't pay tax to the robbing bastard of a government? What and If are unassuming words, put them together and you have a very different situation! My 'what if's' arise once more…

*

The cottage completes in less than 5 days, the Man-Cub is so sad, he is struggling to let go of something that was clearly special to him, it was to me too but it changed, in part driven by isolation and loneliness. The Cub is on my mind. It's a Tuesday evening, the temperatures have dropped and my fire is dying down. I can hear the church bells ringing, they practice on a Tuesday and Sunday. It's a sound I grew up with and perhaps one I stopped noticing until moving away and then returned. It's funny how that happens, you stop seeing and hear what is around you until your environment becomes unfamiliar, then you go into high alert. My home town is familiar, I've just been away from it too long.

This morning I woke early and decided to walk in the park with the dog before getting the train to Leeds. Seeing the Twatterdale running around with such open glee is wonderful. It really is a classic November morning, cool temperatures and clear skies above with low lying mist clinging to the ground. It's so magical and at 7am the sun still hadn't fully risen, which gives the light an even more majestic feel to it. I didn't want to stop walking, I wanted to spend the day outside in nature, something I've neglected to do for months now, due to moving, selling and working. Life I guess! But work beckoned and the 8:04 train had my name on it.

On the way out of Skipton I marvelled again at the light and the flood water from all the rain this past few days. There is more low lying mist which is denser by the river. I don't want to be on this train heading into Leeds. I'm tired, not in my mind or from lack of sleep, just tired of the 9-5pm grind and I'm not being sure of *why*. I made this move so I could start to explore ways of changing what I do, changing my life, the way I live and make time for what truly matters. I can't shake the feeling and for the past few days I've gone over and over my finances to see what I could really live off. Do I seriously need a car? Do I need to spend so much money on food and 'stuff'?

The train pulls into Leeds and I make my way through the streets towards the campus I'm based at. On the way I see council workers trying to remove some graffiti from an overpass. It says "How is your mental health?". I watch the irony of two men doing their best to remove the black writing while a homeless person sleeps beneath the underpass. I can't get my head around what I'm seeing and continue to question what the fuck it is I'm doing here. I get into work and one of the executives is looking for me before I've even taken a sip of coffee. We chat, he talks about wanting to promote me into a more senior post and I talk about wanting to work less. He can't fathom this. He doesn't know what to do with my lack of ambition to climb the career ladder and earn more money. The point is, I genuinely do not want more, well I do, but it's more free time, less stress, less running around and more brain space.

I continue to ponder and wonder if we are kept busy so we don't think. We don't have time to think, just do, sleep and do more. And for who? For what? I call my Dad on the way home and talk about my thoughts. His response is simple; 'I wish I'd fully retired at 50 instead of waiting until cancer kicked my arse and impacted the rest of my life and well-being, do it now dear girl'. Cancer made the decision for him, it was no longer his choice, it was out of his hands. I don't want to hit a point where I sit and use the rest of my energy to heal. I don't know what to do for the best. A friend advises me to take the damn promotion and work part-time on decent money, deep down I know it won't be part-time, the creep will happen and more and more will be loaded on. I know this because not one person I work with actually takes full annual leave and totally switches off. They check in, email, call and are ever present. I don't want to be that person, yet I fear there is an expectation within this subculture which hides behind the shiny one which is projected.

I have big decisions to make, not quickly but the feeling hangs. It's been hanging now for months and I have made progress in setting myself up for being able to have a choice and not be a wage slave. Because ultimately we are all just that, wage slaves who are held in place by consumerism and the flashy marketing that sucks the sleepwalkers into its sticky web. Afterall, if we were truly awake and looked at what really matters the economy would take a hit, a serious hit and the government would never allow that to happen. Let's dangle the carrot, let's keep you in a space where you feel 'safe' but it's not really safe, it's a false sense of security and ultimately a false sense of self.

Instead of passing this feeling by and saying what most people would say "oh well, best crack on because it is just the way it is", I'm going to hold this feeling. Observe it and I'm quietly confident that when the time is right my intuition will tell me what to do. And if that fails I will ask Grandad. If Grandad were here I know what he would say… "Do what makes you happy, don't worry, don't stress because that is no good for you, have faith because it will be alright". He lived until he was 96 and his advice remained constant for me. I'm inclined to believe he knew what he was talking about.

It happened on Wednesday, there was nothing of note, just a call from my solicitor to double check I wanted to actually do this and then another call to say it had happened, contracts had been exchanged. I was at work in Leeds, a busy day lined up and there really wasn't much time to process it fully. But I felt it! I felt this strange feeling of something final, sadness, a bit of wondering how this next chapter of my life would pan out. We often feel reassured by the familiar, waking up to the same sounds, same ceiling and for so many, the same sleeping partner next to them. This has all just shifted for me in the blink of an eye. I no longer wake at 4am to hear my neighbour opening his car and setting off to work or the milk lady putting the bottles on my doorstep. I guess having the ability to move from place to place means that my sounds will change and with that so will I.

I've carried on pondering and it's quite a big thing when you let go of the day to day familiarities, the routine you do so unconsciously. The guarantee of a warm house every morning by a pre-programmed timer, the endless supply of hot water and a fridge full of out of date food. I no longer have this convenience and I find myself being mindful of everything I use, when I use it and my time. Making sure I have time to walk (not drive) to the supermarket and get just enough food for two days. Then plan on what I will cook, how I will store it and if I need to get more ice blocks to freeze at my mums. In just two weeks I have connected to life more and the simple act of walking to get the essentials.

It really is amazing when you slow your pace down and instead of focusing my thoughts I focus my eyes. I've started to notice the habits of people in the park while walking my dog, this would have passed me by completely but now I'm paying attention. The school kids are a blend, some walk in a groups, chatting, laughing, some alone, head down into the wind and rain, the younger year 7 students are still looking for conkers, something which will be so uncool this time next year, this reminds me how my boys have grown and conkers are a distant interest. There is a lone girl, clearly only 11 years old, having an intense phone conversation, with a look on her face which was too sad for a lass that age, I wonder what can possibly cause such an expression. There is the giant poodle who wears a fluorescent orange babygrow for dogs, the owner looking proud and my Twatterdale wondering how to approach such a thing! There are joggers and cyclists, one jogger in particular has my attention. He's dressed in old school kit, in his 60's, wild grey hair and a beard. Every so often he stops, picks up litter, but not just any litter, more specific stuff like a lost glove, a bit of fabric and what appears to be part of an umbrella, he seems to be a collector of things while expanding his lung capacity. I move on.

When I got home from Leeds yesterday I made the decision to start forming new habits. The last couple weeks have seen me come home, often exhausted and go back up to the cottage to pack more stuff. Today I didn't need to do that, it's done, ready, almost vanished. Instead I walked into town along the towpath with a dog that was so excited to see me. Unconditional love. I'd ordered a dress for work which needed collecting, an act I didn't begrudge. I love wandering through the cobbled streets of Skipton on an evening, there is something delightful about it, wet cobbles, reflective light and deserted streets. On the way back I passed a few pubs and decided to stop by one which is popular with boaters, I can't say I go into pubs alone as a rule, however, tonight I made the decision to start to expand my social network and get to know my boating comrades. I stood at the bar and chatted to my neighbouring boater. We talked about the £5000 quote I've just received for a new pram and cratch cover, a potential necessity at a price which has floored me. 'You need a good quality hydrostatic head sheet, it will be just the ticket to and save you some money' said my boating friend nursing his second pint. And just like that, on Saturday morning he is coming to look at the situation and see what might work as a patch job to get me through winter. I feel quietly content. I also know completion day is looming.

*

It happened, I'd like to say there was no drama but there was a smidge. The Drama came in the way of a phone call from the Man-Child the night before completion. He had a buyer for the gypsy wagon and needed to take the dry stone wall down the very next morning, get ramps and manoeuvre the wagon down a 4ft drop and then across a boggy field, now the farmer finally agreed to this! I'm processing. I'd also had a couple of glasses of wine to celebrate the fact that I would never return to the cottage and my little slice of floating heaven is my new and only home. I advised the Man-Child that if he genuinely wanted to get the wagon sold then he had to do this task alone. I also told him he could keep the money, it seemed only fair.

The morning of the completion I woke up after a wine induced sleep, essentially feeling rubbish and remorseful. It was raining hard outside and I knew I needed to hit my job list. A list which consisted of buying a birthday present for my niece, breakfast and handing my keys over to the estate agent. All of which I did without distraction... apart from the birthday present mission. Having two boys and shopping isn't a great mix. Whereas shopping for a 6 year old girl was a different experience. I found myself clutching a pink sequin top with the tiniest pair of skinny jeans you've ever seen! I was in girl heaven, I simply could have spent a small fortune! I then went for breakfast at my favourite coffee shop. As I'm nursing my cappuccino and eating scrambled eggs on toast I get the phone call to say the completion has gone through and the house is no longer mine. I need to hand the keys in asap.

That's it… done. Just as simple as that. I suddenly find it hard to swallow my breakfast.

The lady on the table next to me overhears the conversation and says she too is completing this next week. She asks me where I'm moving to and I tell her I've moved onto a boat. This is something I'm getting better at, expressing where I now live. What I'm always stunned at is the shock from others, which is promptly followed by awe. It's the last bit that amazes me each time. The reality is, there are not many single female boaters or women full stop that bite the bullet and choose to live the life *they* want instead of what is expected, this point is slowly starting to sink in. I am making that move. Correct that… I've made that move. It's done. I'm not sure how I fully feel, well apart from tired, like really tired!

I make my way to the estate agents and hand in the keys, my hands shake and I feel empty. I call the Man-Child and inform him that I no longer own the house and how is the wagon fiasco going? He informs me that the task is done, finished but not without a few hair raising moments! Wind and rain didn't make the job easy and to add to that there were only Two of them. He too then made his way to the estate agents where he dropped the last key off. While the Child was doing that I was on the boat trying to get from one side of the canal to the other to top my tank up with water.

I need to learn that moving a boat in bad weather is a recipe for disaster and doing it single handed is challenging, but I DID IT! This was a triumphant moment for me. It might not sound like a big deal but it actually is. I got back onto the boat, wet, wild looking, covered in mud but with a full tank.

Later that day two fellow boaters came over with a pallet for the roof of my boat. One was tall, rugged and his mere presence made me pause. The other short, chatty with kind eyes. The taller of the two broke off the needed bits of wood from the pallet so it fit the curve of the roof and then plonked it on with an ease that implied strength and experience in those arms of his. I vowed the next day to get my bags of coal up there, clean the roof down and celebrate the fact I now had a pallet on my roof with coal, which makes me a real boater! I chatted with my new found boating comrades and we discussed the merits of scavenging for wood and foraging for mushrooms. I suspect a trip will be in the making to find local hedgerow goodies. I feel excited at the prospect of going to ground with nature and finding the delights it has to offer so that I can rely less on the cash cow consumerism and more on what is right under my nose.

I'm still pondering my next steps and maybe this isn't something which will happen overnight. Maybe I need to enjoy Christmas and welcome in January, perhaps even February and then think about how I can make a living in a way which suits this nomadic lifestyle. Right now I'm processing how to be braver and learn to live off much less money. Boats aren't cheap, the maintenance costs can be a small fortune, I need to keep this real and not run off in my mind with the romantic notion that I can sell books during the summer from the side of my boat and that this will tide me over. But I will find a way, it's just not presented itself yet, but it will!

*

I knew it would happen, I just wasn't sure exactly when it would happen. It was Wednesday morning with warning shots being fired on Monday and Tuesday. Monday was unexpected. I decided to work from my Mum's because I had an engine problem which needed fixing and until that happened I had no power. I walked down the canal with the Twatterdale, pretty happy actually and not anticipating the start of the wobble. I got to Mum's, logged on, looked at my back to back diary and set to work. A few minutes later my Mum brought me a cup of tea. That was it, that was the start. Someone brought me a cup of tea. A gesture so simple that it took me off guard, how sad is that? I felt myself start to wobble but with a meeting looming I decided to direct my attention elsewhere, an art I have mastered!

Working at Mums was a strange refreshing change and I enjoyed it. I wandered back along the canal in the dark and felt quite content when I arrived back at my little boat. I went about my usual task of making dinner, lighting the fire and candles, making it cosy and providing self-nurture. I climbed into bed, my lovely safe nest and settled down with a book and the Twatterdale curled up next to me. I slept. Tuesday was another full day of back to back meetings, a diary with no breathing space and with that I could feel another slice of my energy slip away. I wanted to work from

Mum's again but I didn't even have the energy to get up and get there at 9am, it was easier to stay on the boat, to not move.

By lunchtime I felt angry, sad and wondering what the fuck I was doing. This is not living. I decided to take a lunch break, something I seldom do. I walked the Twatterdale through the park, welcoming the last of the autumn leaves giving their final show of colour. I stopped by a friend's house to drop something off, was invited in for a brew but had to decline because the next meeting was fast approaching. This further compounded my feeling of frustration. I grabbed my favourite coffee, freshly ground from a delightful roasters on the way back to the boat. I was rushing now to get back for the next meeting. Sweat was running down my back, I was dodging people on the towpath hoping that I didn't bump into anyone I know. It was 1.55pm, I'm fretting, the Twatterdale runs off, I'm shouting for her to come back but something more interesting than me has taken her interest. I'm getting stressed, angry and losing my shit.

That night I went out for dinner with friends. Normally a good evening of conversation, laughter and a good bit of British moaning. This time was different. We got into a drop-out row about me not having the Covid vaccine. Three against one and I would not waver, my right to choose, my body, my immune system. I came home feeling more kicked than ever. I poured myself a dram of whisky and sat feeling numb. I slept fine but the next day I dragged myself out of bed, logged on at 7.55am and then the tears came. They came and didn't stop. They had to stop because I had a 9am meeting. I got through until 1.30pm when there was a knock at the window. And there, holding a bag of god knows only what is my Mum. I let her in, she then asked me that question, you know the one 'are you okay love'. And I cried. I also didn't work for the rest of the day.

I called my Dad, told him where I was at in my circle of a headspace and his advice was simple. Take a leap and step off the treadmill. Have faith, it will be okay and go do something which gives me the restorative break I need. I got off the phone, sat for a while and pondered this. I then pondered what was stopping me. What was my fear? Status, ego, fear... it was fear. Fear of not financially managing. Fear of not being able to pay for my bills, my boat, repairs and food. But there was a bigger fear, the fear of losing myself to the system. The grind. It was a genuine fear. I look at my bank account and know I get paid a reasonable amount for what I do, but my heart isn't singing. It's not been singing for months now. There is no sticking plaster, I've tried all of them. I started to pull the plaster off when I bought the boat. To look at a life change, to explore what is possible. What's stopping me from taking off the rest of the plaster and letting air get to the wound?

At 4pm I wrote a letter of resignation. It's heartfelt, honest and to the point. I put my health and sanity first, nothing more, nothing less. I am empty. I've no more energy to give and this isn't going away. And so I have taken the first big step into the unemployment void. The email and text comes back fast from my boss. They offer me part-time with a role I get to create. I need time to think. I take a few days off work because I need headspace. I cry some more. I have until next week to decide. But for now I am going to dry my eyes, take a deep breath and go walk in the woods with the Twatterdale.

Life beyond the cottage is starting to reveal itself, kind of like an onion having layers peeled back. I've come to realise that I've hidden away for perhaps too long, but then would I have grown so much? I'm not just talking about my backside here! I decided to accept a last minute date request on Friday with a guy who I have become friends with on social media. I will be honest, the photos didn't exactly give me any fanny flutters but he seemed like a good egg and so, casting my assumptions aside I took the plunge and said yes to the date. He booked a hotel on the outskirts of Skipton and

I agreed to pick him up so we could go into town for drinks and dinner. He was older than me, but as soon as I met him this became more apparent than ever.

I want to be clear on this, it wasn't the fact he was overweight, which didn't bother me, it was the fabrication of other things early on. Height for example; 5ft 11in, he was actually not a cock hair above 5ft 7in. Type 2 diabetes, not an issue but he brought with him a stash of crisps, chocolate and cider. Overweight but has injections that are the equivalent to a gastric band but keeps eating... Has depression and this defines him, again I have a deep understanding of mental health issues but he uses his as a crutch. Says he's a hippy but is driven very much by money and 'things'. The request for me to wear eye makeup and nail polish... NO. Just NO! I tried to overlook this, all of it at first but as the evening wore on I realised that my respect had totally vanished and I was quite frankly appalled at this man who projects care and kindness but underneath is somewhat manipulative. I can't respect someone who has so little value for themselves and yet has 'a support system' to help them.

Despite all of this the evening wasn't that bad, it actually made me realise that Skipton is a pretty cool place to hang if you know where to go. The first bar we went into was filled to the rafters and I immediately felt I was out with a guy who simply wouldn't fit. The left field moment was the bartender... I felt sucked into this man, which is shameful given that I was out on a date. I realise that I truly do need to go out more. Back to the date, concentrate! He was struggling to walk because his knee needs replacing and has a spinal issue, all due to being overweight. Then there was the sweating, he profusely sweated all night, like really dripping. He went on to tell me he has to sleep in a mask or he stops breathing and has issues with his libido. I was running out of things to say. I found myself getting drunk, something I'm not proud of but it seemed to help. I won't lie, I feel pretty awful writing this, it's unkind and I don't like to be unkind but I felt stunned and misled at the whole experience.

I think the irony is that I'm not actually looking to date, at all! But we got chatting and I thought "why not?" The next morning I woke up and felt so hungover, so disgusted with myself for being nice, polite and entertaining. I'm tired of this crap, really I am. I spent most of the day in bed feeling most sorry for myself and more than anything knowing that I was going to see The Rocky Horror Picture Show that night with my boys at the theatre with the hangover of the century. I needed to eat, sleep some more, shower and get my underwear on so that I could be transformed into Magenta.

Despite me messaging the chap to say, thanks but no thanks, I still got a morning dick picture, which was unprompted, unwelcomed and made me feel sick actually. Why do guys think this is okay? I messaged back saying we needed to remain friends. So while getting my wig on, applying a serious amount of makeup and shimmying into my fishnet tights I get yet more messages.

"Are you okay?"

"Let's chat"

"We aren't done yet"

"I'm worried about you, but have fun tonight"

FUUUUUUUCK OFFFFFFFF! I honestly can't handle any more. Back to Rocky!

My boys turn up, the Man-Child in full suspenders, basque and knickers with a feather bower wrapped around his shoulders. The Man-Cub, a virgin to such things, was dressed as a groupie and looked the part perfectly. The best bit was the fact they were armed with pizzas and I was so damn hungry. We giggled at our appearances and the excitement was building. Hopping in the car, me tottering behind trying to keep up with my boys who were walking in heels way better than me! As soon as we got in the car the sound track was on and the silliness grew! We stopped at my mum's first, who was a great sport in receiving our fabulousness. It was then time to head to the theatre and have a riotous night!

The Cub was about to self-combust with excitement, I was as a parent watching both my boys be who they wanted to be. We parked and the reality hit home that there were hundreds of people dressed in underwear or a costume for the closing night of this mad show. Once inside we mingled, the Man-Child peacocked and the Cub soaked it all up, like really soaked it up. It didn't matter what shape, size, sex, colour or belief you were. It was a level playing field of all bets being off and showing up as your alter Rocky ego.

We took our seats I glanced around and noticed sat behind us, a stud of a man wearing only gold boxer shorts, oiled and oh so touchable. Damn he was fine. Just fine. Sitting there taking in the surroundings of sweat, knickers, glitter, sequins and fun was just the ticket. The Cub was in awe. As the curtains peeled back the noise from the crowd increased 10 fold and the audience participation began. We Timewarped, we shouted, we sang, we did that 'jump to the left' and as Frank sang "don't dream it, be it" I quietly patted myself on the back for 'being it' and following my dreams.

The Cub said he was exhausted after processing what he had just been part of. He said it had been the best night of his life. Ever! I mean, what more does a

Mommatron need to hear? I fell into bed. I sleep the sleep of the dead. The next morning I wake up feeling almost born again and ready to take on the world. As I wander through the park, marvelling at the clear blue skies I bump into my mate Graham who was on his way down to my boat to see if I was home. I did a U-turn and gave him a guided tour. We headed into town where I bought fresh bread from the farmers market and had a coffee while watching the world go by at the pub by the canal basin. I felt happy.

I got home, plonked myself down and buttered the freshly purchased bread. A few minutes later I received a message from a fellow boater asking me if I wanted to go see a band in Leeds? Well... I mean my weekend had been full on and I honestly didn't know if I had the stamina for another session. Maybe I should just do the food shop and have a quiet day. Or maybe I should just throw caution to the wind and go? I don't really know this guy, I only met him a few days ago over a pallet of wood. After Friday's debacle I'm super mindful of staying clear of men and accepting invitations that could end in more disaster. However, I really did fancy going to this gig, and there was something about this fella that made me unable to say no.

The pub is on the corner of a street and looked like it had been clinging onto its dive bar status, all around it were high rise buildings, swanky offices and apartments showing the commercial signs of progression. I hesitated before going in and wondered if I was in the right place, a feeling of trepidation and curiosity was swirling around me like the dry November leaves on the pavement. The windows are old stained glass, preventing you from seeing inside, this only heightens the desire to push open the door and see what is beyond the peeling exterior paintwork. I push the door, I'm immediately met with body heat, the smell of ale and music. This place is a step back in time, I was suddenly 18 again and without thinking I squeeze my way through the tight bodies of pint drinking punters. The walls are dark and grimy, the customers were a mix of leather, long hair, missing teeth, rock, grunge with signs of pure life that screamed from their pores. I looked for my boating mate, who waved at me from across the crowded room, I feel this relief to see his face. Pints ordered. Music pounding. This was like nothing I had experienced in years and years. My feet stuck to the floor, it was wall to wall people, sweat, music and beer. The only thing missing was the thick haze of cigarette smoke.

Drinks flowed. I was in the zone with music and this man whose path I had just crossed and collided with. I found myself watching him, he too was immersed in the music, I'd catch him singing, a deep rasp of a voice, a natural tone of pure blues, a voice I wanted to hear more of. The band were amazing and wrapped up with a blast of Proud Mary, Van Morrison and a standing ovation. People started to leave, we too decided to catch the train home, both drunk, both singing, both lost in a moment of craziness.

The train station is reasonably busy, it's dark and the temperature has begun to drop sharply, I shiver and regret not throwing on a warmer jacket. And then out of nowhere I find myself in close proximity to this man I had spent the last few hours with. He has a voice that is as deep as the ocean and has a way of lulling you into his world just that little bit more, I'm enraptured. His jeans are worn, and have a boater-like grubbiness to them, his 6ft frame topped with faded auburn curls that complement the battered brown leather jacket that is a natural part of him, my stomach turn with butterflies. Without missing a beat he wraps me in his jacket, put his arms around me and lowers his head to mine. I smell the mixture of beer and cigarette smoke on his breath and then I taste it. He kisses me like he knows my mouth and lips better than I do, it's soft and I know that I want more. I've not been kissed like this in years, maybe ever, the sensation runs though me.

We kissed again and again. We get back to our respective boats and go in the opposite direction down the towpath. We exchange messages and I still feel the taste of him on my lips and in my mouth. I shower. I then find myself wandering over to his boat with two crystal glasses and a bottle of whisky. We play music, carefully selected LP's that crackle before the tune fills the boat, we chat, and agreed to stop it there. I don't want to. I want more, I want everything, instead head over heart kicks in and I find myself wandering back to my boat feeling like I've not felt in a long, long time, which was slammed after one hell of a weekend but with a heartbeat that has suddenly changed. Is this what it's like to carry on living after five years tucked away? I climb into bed and reflect on the weekend, the only man that keeps coming back into my thoughts is the man in the leather jacket, cloaked in cigarette smoke with lips that taste of beer and a kiss that makes me feel alive. I remind myself again about not wanting to date, so for now I will keep rolling on a river or a canal in my case. Remaining a Proud Mary and embracing life.

*

Autumn comes to a close, I have less keys, I'm soon to have no job and my youngest son despises me. The boater continues to occupy my thoughts in ways that I can't fathom or shake. My life has changed, my jigsaw puzzle and all the pieces has been thrown in the air and

I have no clue what the new picture will look like or even what my corner pieces are.

I feel a sense of panic but the words of my grandad continue to echo "have faith".

Winter

December is here and the frenzy of Christmas is noticeable everywhere I turn. This year I see a difference though. Despite people rushing around there seems to be a thick coating of melancholy interwoven amongst the glitter and fairy lights. It hangs there, no-one needs to say anything, but you can feel it. When I set out on my journey of unknown change, it was driven by a primal instinct that a fast train carrying challenging times was coming down the tracks. The time is here and now. Now I have slowed down I can see how prices have rocketed and basic necessities have suddenly become something we all keep an eye on, because basic is becoming luxury. I find myself pondering over the price for a loaf of bread and roughly trying to work out the percentage increase from the year before. I need to cut my cloth even more accordingly because my savings won't stretch forever.

I reflect back to September and October and regret allowing the warmth of the sun on my shoulders to lull me into a false sense of security. The forecast is predicting freezing temperatures which means my use of coal and wood will go through the roof. I'm not prepared. I'm now moored quite rural and with the threat of sub-zero conditions, I ponder whether the canal will freeze? Maybe I should have stayed in town?

Maybe my keenness to sail was foolish at this time of year? I speak to other more experienced boaters who all assure me I don't need to worry, the canal won't freeze over. I don't feel convinced, my intuition is telling me to move and do it sooner rather than later. If I stay where I am, I have no access to water, diesel or local shops. Everything is three miles away, irrespective of direction. I go to bed and have a sleep which is far from restful.

The next morning I awake to crystal clear blue skies and a hard covering of frost on the ground. I most certainly need to move! I layer up once a full cafetière of coffee has been consumed and brace myself for the journey to come. In the grand scheme of things I'm not travelling far, 3 miles down the canal and up 3 locks. I've got this! Once the first swing bridge has been tackled I begin to cruise at a higher speed, which is still less than 3mph, my confidence is growing. There is no wind, nothing; the stillness is shattered by the noise of my engine along with the disturbance of the water. Geese ruffle their feathers on the banking and converse with each other as I pass. Once their racket has died down my attention turns to the crunching sound, which essential means the canal has already started to ice over. The temperatures are due to drop further, I feel relieved that I made the decision to move now and not in 24 hours' time. My realisation that my home moves, that I can move and that nature is so close is rather beyond me.

The Twatterdale is highly enthused and zig zags from one side of the boat to another with excitement. We both love moving day, up to now it's only been around a mile or so from the town centre, this time we embrace a real change of scenery. When I move I tend to wake-up feeling renewed somehow, a fresh view and a fresh mindset. We approach the first lock and luckily I've managed to enlist some help for the day. The lock gates are a foot thick, made of solid wood that stands the test of time, water pressure and us bargees occasionally slamming into them. What I marvel at is how nature prevails; plants have grown from the gates and hang like life itself, clinging on, hoping for better times to arrive. I find joy in this alone and it gives me hope that anything is possible, so long as you are willing to grip hard enough. But sometimes letting go and allowing a higher power to whisk you along is also where the magic happens.

The first lock is over with and I sail out of the top gates to be greeted by a new vista, already I feel my soul lift. Breathe. I know this stretch of canal like the ever increasing lines on my face, easy to follow and I do so with little effort or thought. By the time I arrive at the third lock and ease my way in, the gates closing behind, I realise that it is, in fact, still padlocked. I was fully aware that the Lock would only be opened for a two hour period due to essential maintenance work. What I didn't realise was, while the bottom gates were open, the top ones remained under lock and key! And so, I sat there bobbing about on my ship waiting patiently for help, feeling like a true fool for jumping the queue!

An hour later I ease my way out of the lock, hand the lock keeper a hot cuppa tea and mince pie while apologising for being such a keen bean! He was fine, gracious as ever and took the offering of food with a smile. I moored up and began to familiarise myself with the new surroundings. I hammer in the pegs trying to avoid the large amounts of dog poo. It always amazes me that such an idyllic village can have such a staggering amount of dog shit on the towpath. One wrong move and your rope could end up sliding through the unimaginable. Let's not dwell on this.

The next morning I peek out of the window and see that a good layer of ice is now covering the canal. I convince myself that it will be gone in the next few days. The towpath is equally coated and it is this that makes me tense. Walking anywhere when the only traction you have is, well nothing, fills me with dread. Despite the clear blue skies and blazing winter sun, a log burner pumping out heat and a sleeping dog, I feel cold down to my core. I feel excessively tired and find myself counting the days until my notice period is up. I need a break. I need to rest, to sleep late and eat well.

There is no let up. By day six the temperatures are -10, I'm running out of water and the canal is so frozen that there is no chance of me travelling the 70 metres to the water point. The saying 'so close yet, so far away' comes to mind. The boating community is overall very supportive of one another. There is a camaraderie that is hard to find in society today. It is the spirit of this that gets me out of an increasingly worrying situation. Another boater who has a face and voice that has stood the test of time, not helped by cigarettes and weather, offers help. 25ltr drums of water are ferried up and down the towpath until my water tank is holding 150lts. I'm filled with gratitude and relief. This ping pong activity continues for another week, we all support one another and the person at the centre of the activity holds us together like glue. I have to remind myself that looks can be deceiving and under the thunderous face of this other boater is a heart that sparkles like the finest of diamonds.

Christmas week arrives and the ice is starting to thaw. Living off grid is starting to take its toll on me, which is ridiculous since I'm only a few months into my new life. My ego fights but my body tells me otherwise, I need rest. The thought had crossed my mind of checking into a hotel, requesting a room with a bath and indulge myself in some much needed soak. The idea of being cooked for, soaking and reading in a bubble bath is almost too much for me to comprehend, because right now I ache down to my very bones. I cry. I start to wonder if I've bitten off more than I can chew and suddenly I feel the tears roll. I'm feeling lost and lonely. The kettle is on, hot water bottle ready and my bed is calling. Let's see what the morning brings.

I wake the next day, in my stillness I notice the riotous singing of nature has started to quieten and this is becoming more noticeable to me now, winter is truly upon us. I keep convincing myself that I will be absolutely fine, I just need to wrap up and stay warm. Deep down I know that I am kidding myself, I know that reality will bite me sooner or later. This line of thinking took me to pondering over our long gone ancestors and how they prepared for winter. This alone fascinates me. I think of stories my Grandad would tell me about his Welsh up-bringing and the true hardship. He was malnourished, so much so that a few children from the village were sent away for a two-weeks to be 'fed' and cared for in a way which was beyond what his own loving parents could provide. He did have good parents too, this was not neglect which we might assume should this situation arise today. This came from true poverty. For as long as I can remember I would ask my Grandad to tell me stories of him as a little boy. I think this request delighted him as much as it did me. He grew up in Pontypridd, a town in the Rhondda Valley. Even as I say Rhondda Valley, I can hear his soft Welsh accent with the musical tones and roll of the R's.

His two week sabbatical was clearly something that stood out in his childhood, mostly because it involved food. I have been blessed to of had the grandest of men in my life until I reached 45 years old and with that the gift of stories that come from a place of wisdom not knowledge. I don't recall how old Grandad was when he was 'dispatched for feeding' but he did tell me that he 'got a good clout' for laughing at another child. I can't imagine him ever being mean, but then we all have moments when we are young and don't know better.

Here's what he said: "we were sitting down for breakfast, we all ate together no matter what age you were. Some kids had nits, some had clothes on that didn't fit, we were all thin and hungry but that was normal back then. We had porridge for breakfast and the boy next to me began eating his with a fork. He had never had porridge before and didn't know what to eat it with. I laughed and got a clout around the back of the head".

I marvelled at this small insight into life back in the late 1920's when families were large, food was scarce and the 'pit' was your future. Grandad would claim he was thick, that reading, writing and arithmetic was out of his reach. Winters were harsh, with no central heating, no car, no money and only his Dad working. "We would all sleep in one bed to stay warm. My father would put his overcoat over us all to try and keep the heat in.

We didn't mind because it was all we knew. We were happy. I remember my brother telling me there was no Father Christmas, I cried and lost my temper with him. Even Christmas was magical despite us having nothing. If we were lucky we would get one toy and an orange. Christmas Dinner was potatoes and vegetables with maybe a chicken to share amongst us. It didn't matter because we were all so excited. One year I didn't get anything because there was no money. I felt sad, I cried and said to myself, 'boyo, stop this crying'."

It's this that fascinates me. Here I am celebrating my 'off grid life' like it's some badge of honour and yet sharing one bed as a family, having very little food, being malnourished never once phased my Grandad's spirit. Maybe this hardship is what gave him such spirit? I never had the opportunity to ask him how they prepared for winter in those days. Was there planning? Did the foraging for fallen wood begin in September with stockpiling for the harshness to come happen? Was the sense of community greater because the commonalities between each family were the same; that of poverty.

I started to gather fallen branches back in October, with a view to chop them up and store them on the roof of my boat in readiness for winter. My effort was poor.

The nettles and undergrowth were still high and the 'goods' out of view. The few I did find end up in a battle between me and the Twatterdale, who, quite frankly is stick obsessed. Even though I would drag my findings back to the boat and then start to saw them up in between renovations, the task was one I underestimated and suddenly became unimportant. It's hard to prepare when the sun is still shinning and warming your shoulders. I convinced myself this is an unnecessary task and one which will still be there in November... maybe next November.

There is this intuitive feeling brewing and I can't shake it. I feel we are in for a harsh winter. What if I'm not ready, what if I can't hack this lifestyle and all these steps I've made to 'be at one with Mother Nature' get thrown back in my face and leave me cold and humiliated? I can feel my own ego replacing my spiritual soul and the grip I have on reality wavering. I have to remind myself of Grandads pearls of wisdom; "you only have today, there is no point worrying about tomorrow".

It's January, Christmas came and went, with New Year's Eve arriving while I slept. I was in bed by 9.30pm, tucked up with a book, the Twatterdale at my side. I whispered a short and sweet goodbye to the year and asked Mother Nature to usher in a healthy and happy new one. I wasn't interested in observing midnight and the change over from one year to another. I wonder if time is real or just something man made up to make sense of the world? The day is quiet. I've no desire to rush, be anywhere or do anything. I find the increase hype and pressure at this time of year exhausting and vow to be tucked away somewhere remote in 12 months' time. The expense, the expectations and excess all leave me more drained than ever, I'm not even sure what we are celebrating. I think this last few months has finally taken its toll.

My Almanac book begs to differ. The seasons are broken down in such small chucks that you can't help but want to celebrate Plough Day on 9th January. Whilst most of us are sat wondering why our jeans are too tight, our families of bygone days would have been dragging a plough through the streets to celebrate the start of the farming year. When did we lose our tie to what is natural? We seem to be fighting the seasons and pushing our bodies through the harshness of winter when what we really need is to rest and feed ourselves.

Today I was balancing on the side of my boat trying to drag 25kg of coal from the roof when I overheard a conversation between 2 women. "I need to work on my running speed, I'm just struggling at the moment and need to look at my diet to figure out why". I felt the

urge to shake her and say "it's because your body needs to rest, to plump up and be ready for spring".
Thousands of years of evolution have gone by and yet we want to fight it. I see people around me so burnt out and yet the way society is constructed means 'we' just need to push that little bit more.

I reflect back to my not so 9-5pm corporate job from 10 years ago, where I would show up at the modern day equivalent of a Victorian mill. Log on at 8am and if I was lucky, clock off at 6pm, even this depended on whether my manager was still sat at her desk. This is a far cry from how men and women worked the land, ate for the seasons and worked as a community. When did we see food as a natural given and not something that is reliant on Mother Nature and the skill of the farmers? Have we truly been lulled into a false sense of security through the digital age of convenience?

The freeze has gone but the wind and rain have arrived with a vengeance. I still don't feel recharged after the Christmas break, emotions are high and life challenges are even higher. I walk down the towpath carrying a big bag of rubbish, my compass legs are lost, struggling to find which way is north and how to get traction in the unpredictable slide of the mud. The nearest bin is in the village two miles away; I feel thankful for the break in the torrential downpours. I try to be thankful for the life I lead, however, of late it seems there has just been a shower of relentless shite thrown in my direction. In the grand scheme of things I know it's no big deal but right now it feels huge and unmanageable. I feel alone.

I've had a dentist appointment booked for a month now and when the day arrived so did the rain and wind. I was lucky enough to get a lift into town, while I so appreciated this, I had to acknowledge that I had another three hours to pass before the actual appointment. I spent the time going from one supermarket to another, trying to snatch a bargain and make my dwindling money stretch further. My clothes were soaked, backpack full to the brim and no sign of a break in nature's fury. Once the appointment is over I wander the two miles to the train station, I stand on the platform fantasising about Yorkshire Puddings with sausages cooked on a bed of onions and herbs, topped off with gravy naturally! The thought of this keeps me motivated and moving. After a 20 minute wait my train arrives, it's only a four mile journey to the next village and then another two mile walk back to the boat. I now begin to wonder how many Yorkshire Puddings is and acceptable amount to eat in one sitting?

It's hardly worth sitting down on the train, the stop arrives so fast! I step off onto the platform and into the small shelter, gather my bearings and rummage around in my food ladened backpack for the headtorch. I can't find it and with growing frustration I begin to pull all the carefully stacked food out to see if it had made its way to the bottom. After five minutes I realise that perhaps I simply didn't pack it. That familiar lump appears in my throat indicating that tears are on the way. I can't afford to cry right now, it's cold, dark and the wind is picking up as predicted. I sling the backpack on, feel the weight of it on my shoulders and trudge on.

The road back to the boat is a delightful one, it runs parallel with the village, the river creates a natural divide between the two. When I used to cycle, this was undoubtedly one of my favourite routes. It filled me with joy every time I would cruise down the hill and hit the valley bottom, slick tarmac, river to the right, fields to my left. Bliss. Today was most certainly not bliss! The rain was still hammering down and in my naivety I neglected to factor in the rising water levels of the river. Once the village was behind me I was faced with what I considered to be a large puddle. The water was just below the leather upper of my hiking boots, I proceeded carefully and begged my eyes to focus. After another couple of steps the slow realisation crept in, very much like the water which was now at ankle height, this wasn't a puddle. I desperately tried to see further ahead but was met with pitch blackness. At this point my feet were squelching, my boots getting heavier and spirit hitting rock bottom. With the water being at my shins I did contemplate simply rolling over and seeing if the 'puddle' would carry me off home. As tempting as this was, my concern took into account the eggs I'd just bought would also be lost in transit. Finally I wandered under the railway arches with the knowledge that the road was about to rise. There was so much water in the fields that even the dry stone walls were leaking tears of mercy.

I'm home. The Twatterdale is thrilled to see me, but less thrilled to go out for a walk, which is next on my list. I figure she may forfeit her walk in exchange for a sausage, a good deal in my favour.

My PJ's are on, fire lit, wet clothes hanging and food put away. I make Yorkshire Pudding mix, get the sausages, herbs and onions ready and pre-heat the oven. I'm tired down to my bones, I ache, I want to weep and need my bed. The feast is in. With a cuppa tea in hand I plonk myself down on the sofa and breath. The boat is banging against the banking, the wind is reaching 42mph and the rain is still relentless. I check the oven. It's only just warm, not hot like it should be. The gas has run out. I've also hit empty but my stomach drives the one last act of the day, changing the damn gas bottle. I slip on deck shoes and make my way down the gunnels, while holding onto the boat as she fights the high winds. I crouch down on the bow, open the steel lid and locate the spanner. I'm struggling to get enough movement on the bolt which will enable me to attach the gas pipe. After 10 minutes I'm soaking wet (again) and don't feel that confident that the bottle has been attached properly. I hedge my bets and make my way back inside.

Dinner is served, both the Twatterdale and I bask in the fullness of such a simple yet satisfying meal. Today is over. I'm battered beyond comprehension and need nothing more than my bed.

The following morning I pay the price for my lack of due diligence with the gas bottle. The whole thing has leaked out and I'm left with no gas at all. Not only do I forgo my coffee but dinner will also be hummus and celery, not the hot cooked food that my body needs right now. It took another 24 hours to get two new gas bottles. The learning curve continues.

The rain in January has continued with no sign of moving on. Everywhere I look people are trudging with their heads hanging low and eyes to the ground. I overhear conversations about how terrible the weather is, this always makes me smile because winter in Yorkshire is often wet, wild and windy. Yet with each passing year the surprise seems to deepen with the locals. I also see boaters who now have become a familiar sight, albeit hidden under layers of clothing instead of showing off their tanned limbs of summer.

I'm frequently asked how I'm managing, my stubbornness kicks in and with a bit of unnecessary peacocking, I announce that 'I'm fine'. The truth is that I'm not fine and perhaps it is time I simply dropped my basket. And so I let go.

Crying has become a daily act, sometimes more than once a day and this comes to me as a shock. I stop fighting it and see my tears as items in the basket which hit the floor, contents scattering everywhere. I look at the contents and wonder how I have managed to accumulate so much 'stuff' that has been weighing me down. We go through life collecting all these experiences, some beautiful and some bring us heartache; but do allow ourselves to truly 'feel' them? Have we become such experts at surviving that it is easier to squash and suppress the hard stuff so that we can semi function and continue on with these strange lives we have created for ourselves? I reflect back over the past 30 years and acknowledge that I didn't deal with half the life events, instead I compartmentalised, tucked my thoughts and feelings away in fancy jars and boxes because it simply was easier. But now I'm unpacking and all this compressed emotion has come tumbling out onto the floor of my boat and I have no clue where to start with it.

As the days pass my tears become less and the contents of my basket become more manageable. Life becomes more manageable. I slowly decide what I want to gently place back into the basket, what I want to hold onto and carry for a little bit longer. I also start to let go of some heavy items that had crept in when I wasn't really looking. I test the weight of my remaining contents in the third week of January and feel that it might just be okay. I realise that when I let go, drop things and allow the plates to fall and smash, that what I'm really doing is creating space for something new to come on in. There is one item on the floor that remains there, it's been rolling around for weeks demanding to be picked back up and taken on the next stage of the journey. Red wine. Something so simple but so heavy. Despite me not consuming large quantities on a regular basis, the time it has robbed me of amounts to more than I'm willing to give. The same is echoed with Social Media. For now both weigh too much and take up space which could be filled with adventures and possibilities, dreams and love. They stay unpacked.

As the month begins to draw to a close there is a shift. A shift in my heart, my head and the weather. We are blessed with those clear blue skies and frosty mornings with the occasional splattering of snow. I walk the Twatterdale in the morning sun, I'm moored in a secluded spot which gives me views of the river and the most incredible winter sunsets. I start to feel whole again. The frost is so heavy and while madame wanders and sniffs I pause and study. Everyday gifts of nature are suddenly dressed up in their winter finest, all jewelled and glistening in the morning sun. Nothing looks the same, there is a magnificence to blades of grass and seedheads that still remain upright. How wonderful it would be if us humans took guidance from nature and dressed in white? What if we sparkled in the sun with unique patterns that reflect our own individual souls. If only...

In contrast to the mornings, the night sky equally offers up the greatest show on earth with a mysterious distance and depth that is beyond my comprehension. Mars is blazing, the pure red dust of this planet makes it stand out from its counterparts. It reminds me of the towpath in summer; dry, cracked, dusty and warm under foot. The connection from one world to another delights me and my child like imagination.

Somewhere in between dawn and gloaming there is my walk home from a trip to the local village. These days of crisp clarity bring out more people snatching the last hour of daylight before retreating into their boxes of warmth. I dawdle. In front of me are three people of various ages, but more importantly there is the three legged dog. It's back left leg is missing and I find myself studying how he moves, unaware of the absence. His body appears to do nothing to counteract the disability, instead he trots along with an air of confidence, enjoying the trip while seeking out things of interest. I wonder if the dog ever dropped his basket or whether life is too instinctual for him to care?

I reflect on my life changes this past year and realise that the leg I have missing is a corporate one, the professional one where purpose and job titles groom the ego, who am I now? The irony of working for a higher salary to buy more stuff that then needs maintaining isn't lost on me, we create our own cycle, our own life trap. I spoke to a friend today who is pondering buying an air fryer and new microwave with a small amount of inheritance she has just received. I found myself messaging her to ask if those two items would bring her joy or would an adventure leave more of a mark? I then retreat because it really is none of my damn business.

What am I willing to trade for a number in a savings account? Am I willing to trade feeling the sun on my shoulders during the summer, long walks and wild camps for 37.5 hours a week sat in front of a computer? How much money do I REALLY need and why does money give us a false illusion of security? 'Save, save, save', 'they' say but should the mantra not be live, live live? I appreciate there needs to be a balance but is it really necessary for me to be a slave to the machine to feel secure?　Perhaps I need to reframe my mind and seek security in a different form?　Does my security come from freedom, freedom to roam, to sleep late, to wander and dream? Freedom to write, sketch, bake and give time to the Twatterdale?　My children are growing and doing their own thing and already I feel I've missed that critical nurturing window of opportunity.　How much more am I willing to trade for 'stuff' and a number?

When I look deep inside myself and allow my intuition to be heard I know what it says.　It tells me to be still for a year.　To slow my pace, not grab the next shiny thing, but to have faith that everything is exactly as it should be and where it should be.　So perhaps for now I rest easy and let the universe guide me down my path.

The hard frost lasted a week and so did the ice.　On my morning wander I found myself with a heart so filled with joy that I feared it might burst.　It was perfect.　The ice was starting to melt and the pound before the last lock on my way to the village had completely been drained overnight.　It was the strangest of sights, ice in huge sheets and been lowered in line with the water until there was nothing left but gigantic ice cubes.　I marvelled at this, my eyes and imagination were on the canal, while my feet moved without thought through puddle after puddle. My attention was pulled back to reality when I found myself on my back, my left leg at a funny angle and shock setting in fast. Thanks to a passer-by I managed to gingerly get to my feet. The next week has been spent relying heavily on others, while attempting to keep moving in a confined space. Off grid life is now kicking in and kicking me, I feel useless, dependant and feeble.

All is not lost though, as I lay in bed with my leg elevated, I watched the Blue Tits feast from the bird feeder hanging in front of my bedroom window, at first glance it would seem the Blue Tits are wasting food, clinging on with their little feet, pulling out selected seeds from the mix. I marvelled at how much is being dumped on the floor, until the Wag Tails and Robins arrived. Their preference is to eat off the ground and I find a new appreciation for how birds work in harmony with each other. Once bird's is another's gain. Nothing is wasted, not one seed! I wonder if my forced stillness is for a reason? This past month has been a web of challenges, health hits and more big decisions. Is this to make me continue to consider what's important? Who are my fellow bird comrades? I don't have the answer but the question continues to linger.

*

There is a storm raging through at this exact moment, the winds are 52mph and despite the rocking, the howling and rain drumming on the roof, I slept the sleep of the dead, rocked and lulled by Mother Nature. I lay in bed feeling the weight of the different blankets on me, it feels like being held in a warm embrace, safe and loved, there is no need to move right now. I think about the coming season and how animals will instinctively begin to find their mates. Toads in particular begin their flirtatious whisperings round about now. If you are fortunate enough to see this in action, don't be fooled by what appears to be male toad dominance. The male will climb onto the females back and embrace her, this is not to impregnate her, he holds her and protects her from other toads. When she has laid her eggs he will then fertilise them. While my days of egg fertilisation are long gone, what I do miss is the embrace, the flirtatious whisperings and falling asleep with someone's arms around me, legs entangled and heartbeats that never quite sync.

February is moving fast, whereas January seemed to dawdle like a child dragging an over-weight school bag. The days of sunshine earlier in the week seemed to bring people out of their holes of hibernation, I too feel the twinges of motivation to move and explore the landscape where I'm currently moored. With the storm still passing through my drive to leave the nest is dampened, earlier in the week temptation was tapping me on the shoulder. By 11am the gale-force winds are showing no sign of stopping, the rain has retreated and the sun is once again shining and I can't resist the temptation to pull on my boots and go roam. Within 20 minutes I'm out of the door and heading down the towpath, dog at my side, map in hand and an adventure in my heart. I already know where I'm heading, a place where I've not been for 32 years and somehow I know that today is the day. My short stint on the canal is cut short at the first arched bridge, we head over, I marvel at the chunks of stone which create the foundations that must have seen the tread of generation after generation of local people. The Twatterdale squats in appreciation. We both wander on. The track is covered in grass but I suspect that once over it would have been a main connecting route from farm to farm. The mud is reflective of the weather that has just passed through, dark, claggy and unpredictable in depth, this I find out the hard way.

My knees ache, my thighs burn and I realise that I have spent too many months sat on my expanding backside instead of exploring this majestic landscape that is all around me. I vow to myself and the dog that we will breath more, live more and grab what we set out to do with both hands. I cross field after field, easing my way through stiles that are too small for a sheep and if honest, too small for me too! At times I go on my tip toes to squeeze my body through the small stone gap. The green algae coats the stone making it soft and slimy to touch, there is the natural transfer, which has occurred onto my clothes, the deep emerald green fades fast on the fabric, much to my disappointment. My pace is steady, even if I could walk faster, I'm not sure I want to for fear of missing one of those unexpected gifts that nature offers when you least expect it. The visibility is perfect, I stop and sit on a protruding slab of stone that forms part of the next stile, which we need to climb over, both the dog and I celebrate the visual feast that is before us. I know so much of this landscape, I can pick out the contours like the lines on my own face.

We being to climb higher, the wind is stinging my eyes and the strap from my backpack whips my face, bringing tears from the unexpected sting. There is a short stint on a back road, which thankfully is quiet and void of traffic. Before long our climb pulls us up even higher, the bridleway is well trodden and the high drystone walls offer much needed protection from the gusts that I feel I'm battling. While the location of the track is the same, the surface seems more maintained than it was 32 years ago. I'm suddenly 16 again, my whole life stretching before me and the only real care I had was if my boyfriend fancied me, this thought alone makes me cringe. I spent time here in my last year at secondary school, a few of us did but I was the only one who returned after leaving school. My art teacher lived at the top of this hill, it was as wild as she and has had a place in my heart for years. It's only now that I feel ready to stare three decades of change in the face, my main fear is that it's not as I remember it.

The track becomes increasingly rough and I know that I'm almost there when the last cattlegrid is crossed. I feel the rise of emotion after passing a group of trees that are singing in the wind, a noise that is almost deafening. Then suddenly it's there, the row of weather beaten farm houses, the one on the left is what I have my eye on. The sculptures in the garden, are to my relief still standing, these are symbolic with the idyll summer days spent camping in the back garden of my former teacher. I stand still, I have to because the wind is so wild and strong it seems to be forcing me to hold my place for a few moments longer. I walk closer until I'm stood looking at the giant head that I remember so well. I cry. The maternal need to hold my 16 year-old self and give her a thousand drops of wisdom is too much, this whole wave of emotion sweeps through me like the wind that is tangling my hair. What would life have been like with more guidance and nurturing?

I walk through the gate and into the field that surrounds the house, it is all so familiar despite the extension and new windows. There is a drystone wall which has tumbled in several places, failing to keep a boundary between the outside world and this magical haven, I wander besides it, touching it, trying to drag memories back from a time that has long since passed. In the garden the structure of a partially built tower is still there, left exactly as it was all those years ago. I rummage through my backpack for my phone, there is a screen shot of seven young girls sat on the steps of this tower, one with a perm and a 'Pepe Go Wild' t-shirt on. I hardly recognise her as me, I find myself rather longing to climb over the wall just to sit on the step in the sunshine once more. I remind myself that I exist as I am, and that alone is enough, that life ahead of me is more important than a life behind me, which I cannot change even if I wanted to. I find a stone to sit on, I look out in the same direction as the sculptured head, my eyes are the same, everything else has shifted though. I feel truly blessed to of had the creative influence and eccentricity of my former teacher. I suspect that if you spent time in a teachers house now at the age of 16, having a glass of red wine and sleeping over, that front page news would be the only outcome! I have gratitude for this relaxed time back in 1991.

After a while I know it's time to wander on, I cross the field go to the next gate. I'm met with a view of Pendle Hill, rising in all her defiant glory, reminding me that while I have shifted and changed as a person, the landscape has not done the same. I feel blessed to be here, looking across miles of open space, dotted by the occasional farm and distant hamlet. The rest of the walk is stunning, but not quite as stunning as the view from the old house. I continue to cross fields, navigate boggy saturated lanes and try to desperately listen for migrating birds above the howl of the wind. The wind wins. Before long the landscape becomes more friendly, easier under foot and the sporadically placed cottages become more blended into hamlets and then villages. I've hardly seen a soul the whole time and suddenly I know I'm back in rural suburbia due to the number of dog walkers in their 'Hunters' wellies and excessively padded down jackets. I reach the canal, see the flash of colour that I know is home and begin to daydream about a cuppa tea.

Today I heard the first Curlew, it was brief but it was present and I felt a twinge of delight. This winter will be over soon. I've never been one to wish time away but physically and financially I need a break. My back has been firing off warning shots since falling in January, those warning shots have most certainly come home to roost, a bit like the migrating birds! There was no sudden movement, no drama, just one tiny adjustment in the dentist chair while having work done and just like that I find myself incapacitated. I don't use this term lightly and the shock has been somewhat profound, not just for me but those around me. I can barely walk you see, this as you can imagine has turned my world quickly on its head.

The Man-child insists he drives me to hospital, I refuse, convincing myself that in 24 hours all will be okay. Even as the words come out of my mouth I have tears running down my face and know deep down that I'm kidding myself. The Man-child is never one to miss a moment and instead of consoling me further he plays the score from Chariots of Fire, while I try and walk a mere few steps. I love him and despite being in agony I laugh and my tears dry up.

The following day I make the phone call no respectable adult wishes to make, the one where you call your mother and say you need to come and stay for as long as it takes. And just like that I find myself back in my old bedroom after a 30 year absence, gazing up at the familiar ceiling, and wondering what the fuck just happened. I'm on a heavy cocktail of drugs and thanks to this the days pass in a haze of sleep. The Twatterdale is confused and can't quite fathom what is happening, I'm too drugged to pay much attention so, instead I sleep and let Mother Goose worry about her. The hours turn into days and after a week I find myself on less drugs and more able to move with the help of sticks.

My ego kicks in and I feel humiliated at my situation. I don't want anyone to see me like this. I now know how my Grandad felt at the age of 91 when he had to succumb to using sticks. He was highly worried about his street cred and what the people down at the supermarket would say. I feel his pain.

I message my beautiful boating friend, who has been watching over my ship for the past week, to see if he would move her to an accessible place for me, because I'm coming home. There is only so much one can handle when living with elderly people. The night time ritual of going to the toilet in succession, which is repeated between the hours of 1am and 4am, the beige food, TV habits, which include endless game shows. The Twatterdale is beyond anxious and won't settle at all, she too knows it time to flee the nest. The gratitude is there though and perhaps we all need a strange trip home once in a while?

Once I'm back on the ship my movements are still much the same, slow, considered and painful. I also need to think about earing an income, because I have depleted my small amount of savings. Reality bites at a moment when my physical being is on her arse. There has to be another way of earning money while living on a boat, the question is what? I want to embrace this nomadic lifestyle and live like a true bargee. The cogs turn.

The daffodils are out and the buds have made an appearance. Just as I start to get giddy at the prospect of spring the snow arrives. Heavy, thick, coating itself over all the new growth and landscape. I'm desperate to get out and walk but my back has other ideas, I find myself still confined to my 35ft space with a heavy heart and the fear of depression is setting in.

After a particularly heavy night of snow, waking up to clear blue skies and the world iced like a wedding cake, I decide to brave it and take the dog out for a much needed walk. It truly is majestic, the moored narrowboats all pump out woodsmoke from the chimneys, filling the air with the most delightful smell. Beyond this, it's the sound that catches my attention, the sound of clumps of snow dropping from branches into the canal. The rest of the world is bathed in silence and this magnifies the constant drum that comes with the act of melting.

The towpath is quiet, by the time I turn around and walk back home I notice a steady stream of children with their parents, dragging sledges to a nearby field. There is an air of excitement, which only comes with the perfect blend of no school and snow. I climb onto the back of my boat and make a hot chocolate loaded with marshmallows in an attempt to join in the bunking off spirit. It's a piss pour effort. The snow and freezing temperatures stick around for a week before finally giving up and heading on to pastures new and with it I too find myself untying my ropes and heading back down the valley for a change of scenery. I have no real plan but I need to see the arrival of spring somewhere different.

During this period of 'forced paused', I take the plunge and apply for my traders license. I need a side hustle and while I'm not entirely sure what this hustle will be just yet, I figure I will work it out somewhere along the way. In the meantime I put my head back in the sand because it feels safer there. I think this is where I will stay until spring.

Spring
New Shoots

There is that warmth that comes with spring in the air, everywhere I look there are the signs of new life, after what seems to have been a long dormant winter. I now understand why people said I was mad moving onto a boat in Autumn, it has been tough, however, I know there has been no false sense of security that would come with summer. I feel excited about what the change in weather will offer, who I might meet and where I might go. Having less overheads means I have the ability to accept a job I want to do rather than feel I have to do. I find myself working at my local garden centre, a place which has always called my name, with the hourly wage being £9.50 I've not had the luxury of being able to work there until now. Working outside has been a treat, I turn up, follow instructions and get to work. The days feel long and at times very physical, something which my body is not used to, after all I've spent the last 25 years sat at a computer. I also have the burning need to trade from the boat, something I still haven't quite got on with.

I find tending to plants incredibly rewarding, separating stems, pruning and snipping with care and consideration, the slight warmth on my cheeks, soil under my nails and an ache in my legs from standing up all day. I cycle or walk to work, my backpack full of sandwiches, snacks and herbal tea. The team are an eclectic mix, there is no political correctness and the professionalism I'm used to is simply absent, this is an adjustment for me and one that I do welcome because the team and place is real and authentic. I go home at teatime and feel like I have done a day's work, it's physical, and I feel it in every muscle of my body. I also feel grubby and in need of a shower, but first the Twatterdale needs walking and fussing over, for she too has had a long day of waiting for me to come home and the import job of guarding the boat.

The mud on the towpath is starting to dry up and harden, I'm delighted about this because it feels like I've been battling mud for months, not just me but also the dog, she seems to bring in an excessive amount of crap, some rolled in, some stepped in, but it is all part of nature's gift! Whether I'm walking to the local shops or heading to work three days a week, I make sure I'm slow enough to see signs of life awakening all around me. I don't want to miss this arrival because with it will come a summer like no other, this I feel sure of. Now the towpath is drying out I turn my attention to the outside of the boat, all winter I have been trying to ignore the peeling paint, expanding rust patches and my need for some fun colour. The other harsh reality is that my front and back covers have not lasted well over this winter and do need replacing, a bullet I can no longer dodge, I'm also aware of what this will do to my savings.

I begin to set the wheels in motion by commissioning a company to do the cratch and pram cover. At £5000 my bank account has now taken the hit I have been dreading, I'm left with very little and this leaves me feeling anxious. I then need to remind myself that I have no debts , this alone is a positive. The wait time is five months between the order being placed and the covers being fitted, by my reckoning they should be in situ by the end of August or beginning of September. The existing covers are on their last legs and make the whole boat look tired, a look which isn't helped by the existing paint job.

I've never painted a boat before... obviously, why would I have painted a boat before, yet I feel compelled to give it a go. When speaking to other boaters I receive a rich amount of information, much of which is conflicting, with this my own confusion grows and confidence slowly starts to evaporate. I'm six months into living onboard my ship and while there is a staggering amount of learning to do, I find myself willing to roll my sleeves up and get stuck into the grittier side of this nomadic life, which now includes painting my vessel.

Because the information I have received has been so conflicting, including statements like "you need to pay to get a proper job done on this lass, you've not chance of getting a good finish" and "she needs to be lifted out of the water and drydocked, you can't do that on the canal side". All I'm sure are well intended nuggets of advice, what did amuse me is when I scratched the surface with my natural curiosity, the majority of the people offering up this advice had never actually attempted to paint a boat, instead they had paid to have it done or never had the need to even take on the task. My mind is quieted somehow, and I find myself contacting one of the leading manufacturers for enamel paint. When you have no real clue as to what your starting point is, it is hard to know what the right questions to ask are. I bumble through the phone enquiry, hanging up £271 lighter. I also seem to have ordered one of each of the primary colours with no real plan on what the final outcome will be. The pressure seems to be on suddenly.

There is immediate work to be done before the fun of applying colour can commence, first I need to sand her back, in some places back to the steel, a task which I naturally underestimated. I invested in a battery powered sander because I simply don't have enough power on the boat to run a sander, but I do have enough power to charge a battery. I pull on an old pair of sweat pants and a hoodie, choose the most coarse grit of paper and start at the bow end. The sander hits the paint and my heart skips a beat, there is no going back now. Bit by bit the dark green paint fades until I begin to uncover older colours, eventually leading me to the original undercoat. I suddenly feel a deeper connection to my home, I've too have been peeling back my own layers of self-discovery and now my little slice of floating heaven joins me on the journey.

The weather continues to improve and I find myself spending more and more time on the towpath, sanding and then wiping the excess dust away with tac cloths. I peel a layer off and feel the warmth of the sun on my shoulders for the first time since last September, the warmth covers me and I have to pinch myself that this is now my life. After two weeks of sanding one side of the boat, I feel ready to treat the rust patches and then apply the basecoat. I run my hand over the steel, close my eyes and allow my fingertips to tell me what areas need more attention, if only relationships and intimacy were this beautiful. I'm ready to apply the basecoat, I feel a mixture of excitement and butterflies, if I get this wrong I will be back to sanding once again, a thought I cannot face. I pop the lid of the paint and set to work applying the dull grey concoction, it slides on with ease and I congratulate myself for giving this a go. Once one side is finished, I head indoors for a much deserved cuppa tea. After about 30 minutes I go back outside to check the drying process, it has dried to the touch, but what I also notice is that there is an unevenness to the finish, mostly where I've taken her back to the original steel. Bugger...

I call the paint company again and seek more advice, I am assured that once the last coat of enamel goes on, all imperfections will level out, I feel reassured enough to continue. After another coat of paint I decide it's time to turn the boat around and repeat the process on the other side, this is now starting to feel like a slightly larger job than I initially anticipated. The other side goes smoothly, perhaps my confidence is growing and with the sun continuing to warm me through I relax more and more into the task.

While sitting at the side of the canal I find that passers-by continue to stop and chat, ask question after question and at times sit on the grass next to me to engage further. At first I found this an inconvenience, but after a few hours I came to welcome the company, often explaining that I need to keep working while we chat. The steady flow of people traffic eventually got to the point where I put fold out chairs near the boat and made cups of tea for those who had no intention of moving anytime soon. The gratitude amazed me, more than anything I'm beginning to realise that I am living a life people are outrightly curious about. Other boaters come and go too, all continuing to offer advice and critique the work I have done so far, my skin thickens and my knowledge grows.

Before long I find myself looking at a dull, all grey boat and the four cans of paint next to me, I no longer recognise her as mine. I need a plan. Colour for me is important and when I wander the towpath I see boats that often are beautiful but also traditionally safe in their paintwork. I feel the itch to do something completely different, something which will stand out on those dull November days, something which will make people stop and smile. My imagination runs wild and I have to remind myself that painting large cocks on the side will not be acceptable, I'm not talking the feathered kind! I decide to move the boat somewhere more remote before popping the lid of the first can, I want as little foot traffic as possible, as little dust from the towpath from passing cyclists and to also be left in peace to create or fuck up this first effort of painting with enamel. I un-rope and go.

I drift down the canal in search of the perfect location, if such a thing exists? As it turns out it does and 12 locks, one village and one hamlet later I find myself on the most idyllic stretch of canal I've ever seen. It is beyond my imagination, and once you sail under the stone bridge and through the canopy of trees you are met with an undulating landscape and a stagging amount of wildlife, my heart soars. The towpath is more part of the landscape here, rough and unmade, rutty and root riddled from trees that refuse to comply. The banking is a guessing game of where it might start and finish due to the over grown vegetation, some of which consists of Giant Hogweed, a plant I refuse to battle with. There are wild flowers, tiny and delicate cups of blue, pink, yellow and white. Buttercups grow wild against the emerald green backdrop of the rolling fields. It is a true feast for my eyes. I can't stop smiling and find myself slowing the engine into idle, the gentle put put put is a contrast to the bird song, the two compete.

I find a spot to moor, easing the boat into the side, hopping off and tying her up as quickly as I can so I can admire the view. I stand by the drystone wall, there is a gap, a window shaped by two hawthorn trees, I can see for miles, a view of the most spectacular landscape interrupted by the occasional barn and farm building. What I love about this time of year is the excessive brightness of all the colours, the newness of it all and the change in how the air smells. I continue to stand there looking through this natural window at all the life which is stretching below me, in front of me and behind me. The Twatterdale runs up and down, finding something new to roll in and pee on, she too is happy. I pull the folding chairs from the roof of the boat and set them up by the wall, I sit, I watch and I listen, my eyes closed, the sun on my face and nature filling my ears, this will be home for the next two weeks.

The following day I find myself sat back in one of the folding chairs, feet propped on the little wooden stool which seems to follow me from home to home, staring at my boat and wondering what the hell I do next. I look at the cans of paint in front of me and decide that the main colour should be a bright yellow, after all, I haven't seen one yellow boat on my limited travels as of yet. I grab my old yoga mat and use it to squash down the wild grass, nettles and succulents which are growing freely next to the boat. I lay the paint tray, brushes and roller next to me and begin to shake the can of yellow. I pop the lid and marvel at the sheer vibrancy of the mixture staring back at me, it really is BRIGHT yellow. I put the lid back on and wonder if I should opt for something a little safer? The only reason I pause is because I am concerned about what people will think, this thought surprises me somewhat I feel cross with myself for allowing these ridiculous assumptions to guide me decision making. Yellow it is.

When you paint with enamel you must have the perfect conditions, not too hot, not too cold, low wind, no morning dew, and as little dust as possible. I work in small patches, 3ft x 3ft, rolling the paint on and then brushing down to take it off again, a process I repeat until I'm at the stern end of the boat. I sit back and look at the first layer. The yellow has hardly covered the grey and I feel tears coming because it looks shit. Once it is dry I go for a second coat, then a third and a fourth, I count the days with the coats. It is very patchy and I find myself calling the paint company for advice. It would seem that yellow is the hardest colour to work with and I should prepare myself for several coats, with each dry layer being lightly rubbed down if more than 24 hours laps between coats. I realise that this is going to be a much longer job than I anticipated, but one which I need to embrace because there is no going back now.

Seven coats later I find myself looking at one side of my boat which is hardly recognisable and is also staggeringly bright. It has taken the best part of two weeks to get to this stage, I see the summer stretching before me with the act of painting running parallel. A point, which I had not considered is that yellow attracts flies, lots and lots of flies. I have become an expert at picking debris out of the drying enamel, generally bodies only, the wings get swallowed up during the drying process. Once the final coat of yellow is dry, I begin to add blue and red as borders, not straight lines but wavy ones that look like ripples on water. I have no plan, I don't exactly know what I'm doing but my boat now looks like a crazy explosion of colour. I un-rope and move once more.

Despite being moored in a more rural location, the towpath still has a steady flow of people. Some are walkers, some are local, all leave an impression. There isn't a single day that goes by that I don't meet someone new. I have found that since painting the boat an increasing number of people stop to ask questions and engage with an open curiosity. They enquire as to whether I'm an artist, because not only is my boat now a kaleidoscope of colour, she is also starting to be filled with doodles, song lyrics and quotes. I find this level of enquiry hilarious, I am far from an artist, but what I do seem to of discovered is that my boat is a canvas to create on. The Twatterdale's rear end is coated in yellow paint from where she sat in the lid of the open tin! It's all a talking point, a natural level of humour for all those who pass, she unknowingly lets off a generally a good vibe, giving people no option but to smile at her yellow wagging tail.

Some days I sit and watch the foot traffic, it's become a strange pastime of mine and forces me to be still and in the moment. There is the man with the cinnamon dog, he's not tall, I'd say 5ft 6" if not slightly shorter. He wears shorts, t-shirts that are worn and frayed with a hat to cover his bald head. None of this is that important, it's the way he walks that I find curious. He has an air of unexpressed anger, like he's carrying something that he can't let go of and it weighs him down like a man carrying a load of bricks up a ladder. He leans slightly forward and his steps scream the need for confrontation or perhaps a conversation? We've exchanged a few high level passing comments, the first of which comes from discussing how to get a sheep out of the canal. We both wonder if the wool is weighing the animal down and if it is this that prevents the sheep from heading back up the green pastures to her friends, none of which seem overly concerned about one of the flocks dilemma. With this interaction I quickly learn that he's from 'down south', he has very blue eyes and over the coming weeks I find myself grappling with an emotion that switches between anger and sadness at his view on life. The more he shares the more this feeling grows, I also realise that we all have so much we carry and that perhaps our 'bricks' bear a different weight for each of us.

Another frequent fixture in my new place of mooring is the mum carrying her toddler on her back in the rain and drizzle, she has an inner beauty that most certainly left its mark on me. I find myself wanting to carry on talking to her, she is interesting but also had a rare kind of openness to her that you don't often find. Her nose was pierced, she wears a silver feather on a piece of leather around her neck and a ring on her thumb. Freckles dotted her face, tanned, natural, lovely. The child clambers down and proceeds to jump in puddles, blue wellies on his feet with a red waterproof onesie. His face is round, chubby with curious blue eyes, he stares at me with brief interest but then goes back to the puddles, which are far more satisfying. Their dog wanders onto my boat, eats the Twatterdale's food and makes herself at home, while we chat on the towpath. The blue eyed child gets restless, it was time to go. I see this wonderful trio over and over again, each time I marvel at their relaxed sense of joy.

On a casual Wednesday, while drawing a fish on the side of my boat, a tiny lady, no more than 5ft if not less paused for a chat. She has grey hair with a splattering of black, which flew wildly in the wind, you could sense this was her halo of pride and a reminder of youth. She most certainly marches to the beat of a different drum and I suspected that she is a lone woman who loves nature more than any other human, the air of being slightly disconnected from humans radiated off her. She passed comments on the colour of my boat, ignoring the Twatterdale, who was wagging her tail desperate for attention. Without missing a beat she proceeded to tell me about her quest to find kingfishers and how she will spend hours sitting in one spot, in the hopes to see that flash of blue. I do understand the fascination because they are a sight to behold and I find it hard to believe that such a colour exists in this world. She talks for 10 minutes about why staying still and just watching is essential, and how much is missed when we are constantly on the move. I agreed and it did make me think about my own habits once again.

The lady with the collie dog who wears a hat, jacket, jeans and is wrapped up irrespective of the weather is fascinating. Despite me being in a two mile location to her stomping ground over the past four weeks she never speaks. There is no acknowledgement that I exist and her dog reflects her behaviour and body language, minus the hat, coat and winter clothing. I almost want the challenge of the interaction but decide to respect her need for solitude.

This stretch of canal has become my playground, it would seem. I move the boat again after filling up with water, moor up with a new view and proceed to set my painting stall out for a creative day on the towpath. This new location brings the surprise of bumping into an old childhood friend, who plonked herself down on a chair and chatted to me for a couple of hours on this sunny morning. The conversation was a delight, we reminisced and exchanged notes on the last 33 years. She hadn't changed a bit and had led a life, which was akin to my own. There was a wonderful connection and agreement on global events, it was refreshing and it filled my heart for the day.

Yesterday a more mature lady with the kindest face stopped on her bike to admire the boat. I immediately felt at ease in her company, she radiated joy and beauty. She too used to live on a boat until last year, her residence now is a portacabin which is kitted out to be a functional basic home. We discussed how 'people' are brainwashed into thinking they *need* so much and how security is found in bricks and mortar, not each other or from within. I need more time with this incredible creature, I simply want to bask in her glow and hear more about the life she has lived. The invite was open and mutual. She cycled off with her skirt flowing behind her.

In complete contrast was the Rolex watch man. I was still painting when he stopped, not to admire my handy work but to lecture me on boat painting, I brace myself for another lecture off someone who has never actually painted a boat, in fact doesn't even own a boat! I found my tolerance for him dipping with every passing second he invaded my space. I found myself getting ruder by the minute, I wanted him out of my tranquil place, I felt like he was contaminating it by just breathing the same air as me. He eventually moved on and my lungs expanded with a sigh of relief.

Some experiences plonk themselves firmly in your mind, recently two ladies at the more mature end of the spectrum walked past with purpose, we chatted, laughed and they asked me questions about my life choices. About an hour later they came back again and enquired as to which way they should head in order to get to Gargrave. These two birds had been walking in the wrong direction for the past 6 miles! I invited them to sit down on the folding chairs, put the kettle on and brought out tea and biscuits. These were consumed with gratitude and followed by the need for the loo! I find such joy in meeting women who wander, who have lost their life partners, have children that have flown the nest and how they find happiness in friendship. I'm always curious about the commitment to their lost love, wedding and engagement rings still in place. Memories still on the tip of their tongue.

The string of Pennine Way walkers on this one particular stretch of canal is a joy to watch. There are no conversations that take place, just a fixed line for a mouth, heavy backpack and a determination set in their eyes. What should be a joy seems to be a chore and my itch to engage with them is as strong as ever. I often chose not to, they clearly have somewhere they need to be.

Some of my conversations don't take place on the towpath, some take place on the water with passing paddle boarders drifting past and stopping to natter. All of these people have their unique path they are following, their own reason for being in a particular spot at a particular time. Some warm my heart, others make my blood run cold, all remind me that we are unique.

*

With the firm arrival of spring I've noticed that all the
boaters come out of hiding and real movement on the
cut begins. By now I've exchanged waves with many of
the same people and the familiar tribe of bargees have
become part of my new travelling life and me theirs. I
still think about the 'Proud Mary' moment, nothing
more every came from that kiss, wrapped up in a
leather jacket on the platform, much to my
disappointment. We still exchange words when passing
though. I was moored up near him a few weeks ago and
came home in the pitch black to see the distant glow of
a cigarette on the towpath. I craved a drag despite
being a non-smoker. I don't know if it was the cigarette I
craved or to taste him again. How can one man leave
such a lingering mark on my soul after such a brief
encounter?

Winter made me realise how single I am and as much as
I would like a partner in crime, I realise that I have
perhaps limited my options with my choice in living and
lifestyle. I've also realised that the older we all get the
more baggage we carry, the kind of stuff that pops out
when you don't want it to. Maybe I am destined to live
a single life being the captain of my ship, dog in tow,
music on and freedom in my heart. But how nice would
it be to share a beer, sunset and a fire on the towpath

with a man who loves me as fiercely as I love him? How nice would it be, to be someone else's red glow on the towpath? There is a line in the song Uninvited "like any hot blooded woman I have simply wanted an object to crave". Maybe *he* is the object that I crave, I crave it because I can't have it. It's an unfortunate slight and despite the crossing of our ley lines being brief, the term 'unrequited love' pops into my mind.

All winter I have kept myself tucked away, remote, secluded behind the pulled down blinds. I now find myself drifting into town with the relentless encouragement of the growing tribe of boaters that seem to have become a kind of family. We all have this unspoken energy that comes with spring, you can almost feel it in the air and between us. I'm not sure what it is exactly but I finding myself saying 'yes' to mid-week parties, to food, beer, whisky and a rolled up cigarette. Who is this person? Where has the other version of me gone and who is the real me? I feel I've drifted into another world, one which is marginalised unless you are within it.

My legs are starting to turn a golden brown with clear cut tan lines from living in shorts. I'm relaxed, I sleep deeply with no alarm to disturb my wild and crazy dreams. My compass that normally points due north has lost its magnetic field and instead spins around wildly without direction. This is now my life.

Tea with the man who wears the burgundy boot cut corduroy's has become a regular fixture. He too is new to boating and is finding his feet. We never drift far from one another, always within a stumbling distance, which facilitates our alcohol fuelled sessions, filled with music and conversation that rarely stays on track. He is my boating comrade, it's non-sexual, purely platonic and delightfully comfortable. We take turns in cooking and hosting, it always starts civilised but is guaranteed to end in slurred words and focused calculation when getting off our respective boats. The following day we lay low, both nursing hangovers with a reluctance to leave the safe confines of our nests. I find myself vowing not to drink again and question how my life has so quickly spiralled out of control?

The weekly trip to the laundrette sees me dragging over-full bags of grimy clothes that have been worn more than once and are in desperate need to be cleansed. Maybe it is my mind and soul that needs cleansing, it seems to be sliding further into unrecognisable activities with each coming week. I ponder on life at the cottage and how wearing a pair of jeans more than once was inconceivable. I now find myself wearing the same pair of socks for three days or until the shame kicks in, at which point they are tossed into the laundry basket, a hole that has scent all of its own.

While loading the washing machine my attention is drawn to the man next to me, he is one cycle ahead of me and is emptying his fresh load into a bag, which he then drags across the floor to the dryer. We exchange glances. I secure the door of the machine and go perch on the low yet deep windowsill. He joins me and sits to my left. To my right is another man in a dirty orange jacket, his hair matches the colour and I can't help but notice his dishevelled look. The three of us strike up a conversation that quickly reveals parts of who we are as people. The man to my left lives in a van and the orange jacket man on a boat. We are united by our lack of mains living and begin to share the brief but deep narrative of why we are living off grid, unplugged and free. The conversation turns to covid and the absurdity of masking wearing and compliance driven through fear. Despite the fact that two years have passed, the three of us find ourselves processing the fallout of this historic time. At that moment a couple walk through the door wearing black fabric masks. The timing was impeccable and the three of us exchange knowing glances, there is no need to use words, because there simply aren't any.

Even though the van man's load in the dryer has finished, he sticks around and chats. It's an easy conversation that goes beyond the boundaries that you would have with people who live a more mainstream life. 18 months ago I would never have conceived of going to a laundrette and now I find myself looking forward to this weekly ritual, not because I enjoy doing laundry, but because I value the anticipation that comes with knowing I might meet someone new. Someone whose mind can expand that of my own, even if it is just for an hour.

The water levels in the canal continue to drop due to the lack of rain, rumours of movement becoming limited begin to circulate like a steady drum beat up and down the towpath. If the locks are going to be closed I need to ponder where I want to spend the coming months, town or countryside? The decision is not one I dwell on for long, I know exactly where I will head and I suspect I will need to make the move sooner rather than later.

I chat to other boaters, test their thoughts and plans, especially the more experienced ones, after all, I'm still a novice and sense the value in having the opinion of more worldly travellers. One boater I know has a tendency to not move far, but wherever he moves his presence is known. There tends to be a sprawl of 'stuff' on the towpath, which is an overspill from his boat, a boat that holds an eclectic mix of items usually found in a scrap yard. What I delight in, is that he truly doesn't give a shit and is a bargee through and through. There is a sense of old school living with him, which keeps the 'posher' boaters at arm's length. He has a charm and can hold a conversation that varies in depth.

My days can often be spent talking to other full-time liveaboards, our paths cross consistently, we know each other's dogs and general habits. There are the boaters who hold their homes together with tape and fly sheets and those who shine their portholes each week and sail to empty the cassette toilets instead of walking down the towpath pulling their weekly load of shit. There are some of us who venture to the laundrette and those who boast of having a washing machine and dishwasher! My biases kick in and I find myself becoming judgemental of the class system that has made its way onto the canal. One boater said to me in recent weeks "you don't want to end up like these scrubbers, make sure you work hard and hold down a job". The comment stuck with me for days after. It niggled me and made me question my lifestyle choices. Am I truly being delusional about craving a different life that doesn't revolve around a 50 hour week and climbing the ladder professionally? Will I end up on my arse a few years from now? I feel anxiety for the first time in months.

I turn the negative 'what if's' around in my head and then decide to package them up and pop them into storage. Tomorrow isn't a guarantee and I don't want to live in a future that hasn't yet happened. I chat this through with the Twatterdale, who in her scruffy glory wags her tail in agreement. I pull on my trainers and we go for a walk in celebration of this present moment.

*

With the sun higher in the sky there is less need to run my engine, the solar panel is working it's magic for me. I'm relieved to save diesel, especially given my worrying financial situation. On occasion I decide to use the shower blocks that are placed at set locations along the canal, it saves on my limited amount of power. I slip on flipflops and make my way down the towpath with a bag for life stuffed with fresh knickers, towels, and general body care products. Knowing that the shower is used by many other boaters makes me twitch at first but I soon get over this by linking the task at hand with a swimming pool.

The key jams in the door and I find myself forcing my way in and then struggling to remove the key from the lock. I finally manage it and then remind myself that I have to lock myself in so other boaters don't happen upon my 48 year old body. The room is cold with one chair in the corner and mould on the ceiling, I'm thankful for my flipflops. I turn the shower on and wait... the water trickles out like a stream during a dry summer. I play with the dials to try and bring some heat into the freezing drizzle. I'm naked, cold and becoming frustrated with the fact that there is no correlation between the temperatures on the dial and what is coming out of the shower head. I eventually manage to get a reasonable temperature, something, which doesn't hold for long. The water ranges from scorching to freezing in the space of seconds and my two shampoos and a conditioner happen in breakneck speed.

Once the cleansing task is finish I dress, trying to pull on my jeans without getting them wet since the floor is now flooded with no sign of the drain doing its job. I find the whole episode amusing and feel like 'I've arrived' in the boating world. One dressed I leave the small concrete block and wander back down the towpath with a towel wrapped around my head, much to the amusement of the village dog walkers. It never crossed my mind that this look was not exactly normal!

As I'm unzipping the back canopy another boater approaches me and we strike up a conversation. He's slighter newer to this lifestyle than me and we exchange the learning curve that comes with this way of living. The chatter drifts to music, he plays bass and we discuss a mutual friend who is an excellent fiddler. It is this that makes my heart swell, that within the eight boats that are all moored stern to bow there is an abundance of creative talent. Behind me is the blacksmith who works and trades from his boat, a fiddler, a bass player and me, who has a harmonica that is still untouched. I love music yet play nothing, perhaps the tides need to change?

The fellow newbie boater offers up a wander to the pub the following evening, one I readily accept because I am keen to delve deeper into conversation with him and the fiddle player. There is the murmur of another bargee joining us who plays the squeeze box. How utterly delightful and unexpected, which I think is starting to sum-up boat life!

Stepping away from the professional world has been an eye opener for me, I feel at this point my eyes are pinned open, perhaps never to closed again. The minimum wage world is a different one to what I'm used to, my bank statement is analysed a few times a week now, in the hopes that what I'm seeing isn't real. I keep waiting for a large salary to be casually placed in there on a set date each month. Working at the garden centre has been such a treat, but being outside in winter and early spring, while living off grid has taken a toll rather quickly. My ego feels dented, not helped by falling and damaging my spine. As much as I love pulling trollies of plants around and having my hands immersed in soil, I know my physical being has other ideas. With a heavy heart I drop my uniform off and resign myself to the fact that I have work to do on healing my back.

My reliance on the boating community hasn't dipped, the fear of lifting anything heavy is enough to make me stop in my tracks, I simply can't do it. The other frequent quandary is moving my boat and bringing 15 tonne of steel to a stop using only my body and a rope. I can't always get the support I need when I need it. I despise the feeble feeling I get every time I have to ask for more help. What I find in this floating community is that everyone is happy to help and truly sympathetic to my current situation. I am humbled. My back shows no sign of returning to its normal self and I know it's time to face another reality.

For the first time in my life I need to claim benefits. I have fought hard against this for weeks but realise that my £391 isn't going to last me another month. The film 'I Daniel Blake' could not be truer when it comes to the battle you have to squeeze even a drop of money from the government, a government I have paid into for 30 years. The staff are helpful, the system is not. It's cold, impersonal and void of any real support to help with basic necessities. Throughout winter 99% of the population received a £400 heating and fuel allowance, yet because I live a nomadic existence I qualified for nothing. The inequality is astounding and unquestioned. The time lapse between applying for benefits and receiving anything is around six weeks, in this time you attend meetings, phone calls and are under tight scrutiny about your situation, because after all, maybe I'm just here to screw the system!

While being subject to fighting for £334 a month, which is the maximum limit I can claim I find myself shifting between moments of panic and calm. Somewhere deep down inside I know that I'm on this path for a reason and that I must have faith in the Universe, a faith that at times shakes and is clouded in doubt, yet it still holds on and quietly reassures me that everything will be okay.

The trips to the supermarket are slow and calculated, I find myself holding a bag of couscous and wondering how many meal variations I can make from these tiny pasta grains. I watch other shoppers with loaded trollies, stacked with alcohol, ready meals and highly processed crap, I'm not sure I would swap my basket for theirs even if I could. Even on my staggeringly limited budget, I still vow to eat as well as I can. I've become a master of making food stretch and my culinary skills really have come into their own. The foraging for wild garlic continues before spring turns into summer, I make pesto, which is a cheap and delightful combination with pasta. I feel at one with nature because of this.

I find myself lying in bed in the early hours of the morning, the twatterdale heavy at my side, blissfully unaware of the financial situation. During these hours of not sleeping, I read, soaking up the words of Walter Greenwood's 'Love on the Dole', a book I stumbled across on a pile at the local supermarket. I savour his every word and realise that I am not experiencing true poverty. We have so much and yet so little. Having been brought up in a single family, council estate and limited education myself, I can connect easily to the working class roots that Greenwood writes about. My fight to escape this generational 'hand me down' existence has been vicious and yet here I am, on the dole minus the love. I reflect on my need to prove myself and find so much comfort in knowing I no longer need to do this, I have succeeded and made a conscious choice to step away from the middle class trappings. I ask myself quietly how I 'feel' and realise that despite living with a huge amount of financial uncertainty and being at the mercy of the government purse strings, I am happier than I've been in years. I try to make sense of this revelation and the only line that comes to mind is from Bob Dylan's song 'Rolling Stone'; "when you've got nothing, you've got nothing to lose".

When I walk into the Job Centre, a place so unfamiliar, I'm met first with a security guard and then other people sat in cubicles that aim to give poor privacy as you defend your out of work situation. I want to cry because this truly is the other side of the coin, a coin that is judged with biases from those who eat the greener grass on the other side of the fence. I'm now grazing in the same paddock with the people I before couldn't understand or related to. I begin to justify my existence along with the other cubicle dwellers and count down the weeks until £334 arrives in my void bank account. I need to do something to remedy this situation.

The quotes and images on my boat pull a natural crowd and I realise that it is time to seriously invest in a trading license. The associated costs are put on a credit card, an act, which at first upset me but now no longer bothers me. I begin to create and paint a small batch of greeting cards, coasters, plant markers and other goods that can be sold at the water's edge. I invest in 5lt thermos flasks, paper takeout cups, an A-board and food safety qualification. It all costs money, money I don't have, yet I am willing to try this side hustle with my biggest fear being public rejection because my work isn't good enough. I have to find the courage to stretch beyond this limiting mindset because if I don't try I won't ever know. I'm crippled with self-doubt and feel the need to head to the hills for a much needed think.

The Man-child flew the nest a couple of weeks ago and now resides in the place that fills my heart and soul… Wasdale. He works and lives at the Inn up there with the dreadlocked goddess I met months ago, it feels like a lifetime ago. I miss him desperately, his energy and light feel too far away from me and selfishly I wallow in this. I have one eyeball on the forecast and see this beautiful window of opportunity to do a drive up and visit. Because my sister has never ventured on to the fells, it feels only right to extend the invitation to her as well. Thankfully, she readily accepts with the caveat that she is 'unfit'. I always have this quiet belief that we can do way more than we imagine if we just put our minds to it; I carry this thought with me and ponder what route to take her on. The excitement builds, in part because I get to see the Man-child in my favourite place and because I get to drag my sister up a mountain! What could possibly go wrong?

The journey up to the Lake District was filled with chatter and giggles as I navigated Hardknott and Wrynose Pass at full throttle in my Fiat 500, in the hopes that she didn't get stuck half way up one of the 33% gradient hairpin bends. My sister seemed to clutch to the side of her seat for dear life and was thankful when I pulled over for a roadside wee between the two passes. On the descent down Hardknott the brake pads were letting off a smell that I desperately tried to ignore, failing miserably due to my sister pointing out the obvious stench.

The road eventually becomes slightly more tame, with an easier undulation creeping in. Before we know it the cattle grid is crossed and the majestic fells that embrace

Wastwater are feeding my senses. I pull the car over and both my sister and I get out to take photos of all the 'greats' that welcome us. I feel like a child in a sweetshop, I want a little bit of everything all at once and yet I feel acutely aware that my body is no longer able to fell hop like it used to. I bundle my sister back into the car and take the beautiful single track road that runs alongside the lake to Wasdale Head Inn. We pull up and while my sister is faffing with shoes and layers, I stop and stare at the grand presence of the mountains all around me.

We head to the side door of the pub, I push it open and know without even looking what will greet me. As always, it is like coming home, only this time my boy is there to welcome me in. I hug the Man-Child and my sister does the same. We discuss the plan for the day, one which I had been quietly mulling over while swinging my car around the passes. I announce that I plan to take my sister up Lingmel and potentially down the corridor route. Eyebrows are raised and questions asked, not over my ability but how my sister will manage on what can be a challenging route. I brush these off and give reassurances that I will make a decision once we hit the cross point just before the summit of Lingmel. I push us out of the door before more questions are thrown and minds are changed. The walk begins.

As with any wander, I find the pace in the first quarter of a mile slightly up tempo, a tempo which rapidly changes and is always set by my walking companion. I resist the urge to slow people down when they set off and know that this will naturally happen once the reality of the walk sets in. The standard donkey path up Scarfell Pike is well pathed to accommodate people who come from all over to climb the highest mountain in Britain. It is my least favourite route in the whole of the Lake District. Not because of the views, which are naturally breath taking, but because of what I see in people. Not on this trip I might add, but previous trips, where the sheer volume of people resemble an isle at the supermarket, stacked with turkeys at Christmas. People battling for their place on the path, checking their Garmin to see how fast they can ascend, all the while missing the beauty which surrounds them.

Today was different, there were no people in flipflops, there was no smell of weed or groups carrying cans of lager, just a steady stream of people all coming down. It was this that made me pause and check the time, the afternoon was dwindling and we were the only people heading up the mountain. Under normal circumstances this would not have phased me, however, my sister's pace was slow and steady, and this must be taken into my account when making decisions on how we descend.

At regular intervals I force flapjack down my sister and encourage her to keep her energy levels up, I knew she was struggling and felt real anger at myself for underestimating her fitness level and pace, I know better! By the time we hit the cross section at the foot of Lingmel summit, I hit her with the options. We either go back down the way we came, summit Lingmel and head down the steep grassy path or do the corridor route, which arguably will be challenging. My sister tells me what she doesn't want, which is to go back down the way we came up, this I agree with. I suggest Lingmel as a summit, but the look on her face tells me the thought of climbing higher is off the table. Which leaves the corridor route as the remaining option.

I had my reservations, more because the route is thrilling and would push her boundaries beyond where they already were, which was teetering on the edge. I'm blunt in my delivery of what to expect, and enquire about her comfort with heights and scrambling. She convinces me that she will be fine, and so we proceed. We hit the first narrow ledge where the path becomes questionable, drops more aggressive and the gaping black slit of Piers Gill visible. The salmon coloured rock is dry and dusty, smooth yet sharp and cool to the touch. I'm in my element.

I go ahead slightly and give my sister instructions on where to place her hands and feet if she is in doubt, I carry the kit and feel mindful of my centre of gravity. She is doing well. For the past 45 minutes I have had my eye on two black clad figures who seem to have been zigging and zagging with a randomness that concerns me. We are now suddenly looking down on the two figures, who are crying, shaking, and begging for help. I tell my sister to find a safe place to sit while I climb down to the ledge they are sitting on so I can assess the situation.

The two Chinese students had been out since 7am, are exhausted, have no map and no real idea of where they are. Their request was to get the bus back to Windermere and call mountain rescue with immediate effect. I persuaded them that mountain rescue was not necessary and that once they were calm enough to move, I would get them off the mountain and back to Windermere. Suddenly I was responsible for three people and a dog, I go to a space of calm in my head and think about daylight hours, ability and the route head.

Over the next four hours I ease three tired and hungry people off the corridor route and onto the apron strings of Great Gable, a path that will lead us down to the pub where I know my son will be worried sick. The students are shaking but follow the instructions I gently throw at them, my sister cries and more food is forced her way since I know her energy levels must be depleted. The light is stunning, the setting sun casts a glow like no other over the surrounding fells and despite the situation I find myself soaking up the visual feast that is this valley. The descent is slow, the scree is on the move and my exhausted sister slips and lands on her back before I can do anything to stop her. She lays and cries, something which needs to happen. I kneel down next to her and give her words of encouragement that she has achieved so much and should be proud of herself. I also need to get her back on her feet quickly because the sun is dropping behind Yewbarrow and with it the temperature will plummet.

She manages it, and so, we all begin to move, one tearful sister and two Chinese students who will likely never venture on a mountain again. The cottages at the foot of Kirk Fell are there to welcome us, the light has gone but I feel a sense of security in knowing that the pub is 15 minutes away and the ordeal is over. The students slow, my sister slows and the Twatterdale continues to be at her heel, an act that surprises me, since she is normally off venturing. The blue hew of the night sky is awash with subtle colour if you look carefully, all set against the backdrop of the fells, which now form a black outline and seem more forbidding than ever. The stars put on an amazing show, I turn around to find the students staring in wonder. I study their tired faces and wonder what it is they are thinking? My question is answered.

"In China we live in a second class city, we have never seen the stars like this."

I find it hard to believe that the beauty I sometimes take for granted is for some like opening their eyes for the very first time. We all stand there and cast our eyes to the heavens. We are silent.

Once we enter the pub I am met with a concerned Man-Child, who was about to raise the alarm for Mountain Rescue. He knows my habits, he knows I would seldom come off a mountain in the dark. Beer is poured, food is ordered and appetites are lost. It's 9.15pm and I know we need to get moving in order to hit Windermere and then get home. I hug the Man-Child, I don't want to let go and feel sad that I need to return home so quickly. I vow to be back but with the Man-Cub at my side next time. We exchange our goodbyes and I load three people and a dog into my Fiat 500 and set off on a drive that seems to last a lifetime.

I eventually pull up near the boat at 1am, I'm past tired, I'm past processing the day, I want my bed. I crawl in, the Twatterdale takes to the sofa where she stays for just under 24 hours. Her reluctance to move confirms my feeling that we have both had one adventure too far. Tomorrow is another day, hopefully one filled with peace.

*

I pulled my finger out and traded off the boat for all of two days and felt nothing but anxiety the whole time. The feeling threw me, I didn't see it coming but the sudden invasion of my home and incessant questions became simply too much. By the Tuesday morning I found myself sobbing and looking at a photo of my Grandad and asking "where are you? It shouldn't be this hard should it?" I was met with silence. I know if Grandad were here he would have quite simply have told me not to worry and that it will all be just fine, to have faith. Even as I write this, tears roll down my sun kissed cheeks and I feel his absence more than ever.

I dried my eyes and did the only respectable thing I know how to do, un-rope, turn the boat around, and head to a more rural location with views over the fields. And that is just what I did. Normally I aim to have crew with me to help with swing bridges, but today I felt a determination to fly solo and call upon random strangers with children to assist in pushing the bridges open. This task alone was an unexpected delight and I underestimated how much joy such a simple act can bring a child. Before long I was heading through town and out the other side to join the flotilla of friends that were congregating at a particular spot. The welcome warmed my heart and I immediately knew I'd made the right decision.

I moored up in front of the man with the burgundy boot cut pants, apart from today they were cinnamon coloured, something I felt the need to comment on. This was met with an appreciation for the fact I had noticed the new corduroys. There was also an exchange of glances between us in a non-sexual way, glances that meant one thing and one thing only... it was time for family tea and wine. We class ourselves as family now and the ritual of cooking followed by sharing too much wine seems to slot together like a finely carved puzzle. This occasion was no different. The towpath firepit was built and lit, food cooked, music on and the conversation flipped from topic to topic until neither of us could make sense of anything. I knew control was lost the minute the bottle of whisky came out, the unravelling was irreversible along with the digestion of my dinner, which ended up reappearing into the canal, much to my shame.

The next day was a quiet one, one where I needed to assess why I felt the need to get so utterly drunk, and think about how I get this under control before summer really kicks in. I also realise how much I've let go of controlling every situation, and how much my life was within set boundaries of social acceptability. Being on this stretch of canal with friends feels safe, but it also highlights how rife drugs and alcohol are with some lesser known bargees. Three nights later more boating friends congregate around the fire once more, and as the beers flow, so do the stories of a misspent youth from each and every one of us. Age range varies within the group, and this is expressed through the beautiful narratives that spill out onto the towpath. Stories of three men to one woman in a particular town, endless parties, home brew, 1980's poverty, drugs that hadn't been tampered with and the joy of sharing a can of Special Brew in the park as part of a night out. So much of this was beyond me, yet watching the animation on the faces of each story teller sparked my imagination with visual imagery.

The playlist was rotated amongst us and with it songs of each of our youth were sung and acknowledged with merit. We were wild, unbridled and damn right free. Is it possible to feel so lost and found at the same time? The question is fleeting but relevant.

The End or Pause?

I'm not sure what my expectations were 18 months ago when I set off on this journey of having less and gaining more, but it has been one of personal growth without question. There have been times where I have felt joy permeating through every fibre of my being, while other times have been filled with a despair so profound that the thought of living another 30 years is beyond my comprehension. I have reflected back on life over these 48 years and feel a strange exhaustion and yet my curiosity to know what is over that next hill keeps me going. The people I meet more often than not feed my soul and others make me question humanity, all are part of my journey.

The more off grid I live the more I drift from this strange reality we live in. This world we have carved out around ourselves seems filled with chaos, false security and the assumption of a guaranteed tomorrow. I've had time to be still, to reflect and observe, the truth is, in my opinion, is that we have become so far removed from what truly matters. We complain about the price of food, yet continue to fill our carts with over processed crap that we consume without thought or consideration. We abuse the land, our bodies and each other, much of this abuse is carried out through a virtual medium that has become accepted as normal, when it is anything but normal.

In my quest for living a freer existence, I have found a different part of me and seen life through an ever changing lens. I am learning each day to let go of control, to trust the universe in its guidance and be still enough to allow my instinct to speak to me, an instinct, which has been passed with each generation and evolution.

I still grapple with the need for certainty, security and reassurance that I will have paper money or plastic in my wallet to pay for the contents of my shopping cart. When I catch myself fretting over a future that hasn't yet happened, I pause and collect my thoughts. I've spent a lifetime of chasing money, possessions, people, careers and a tomorrow which doesn't exist. I acknowledge that there is a staggeringly high probability that tomorrow will arrive on time as scheduled, however, I don't want to live in next week, next month or next year. I want to live now.

In recent weeks I have felt hopeless at times, some of which was attributed to my health and others to the content of my bank account. Yet when I stop and really think about the situation and look around me, my life is full of the basic fundamentals for human existence. I have food, a home, warmth, clothes on my back and shoes on my feet. I have the love and care of people who have become part of me, an open heart that has so much to give if the respective recipients open their hearts too. What I see and feel all around me are people who are scared to let others in and mistrust themselves as much as those who surround them.

In the past week I've had towpath conversations around a fire with people who hold a special place in my world, maybe the place is permanent, maybe it is temporary, but it is 'now' and that is what matters. I've expressed my restlessness and that I still feel there is so much more to experience in this beautiful world of ours. One boater quietly said to me "you need to get off the linear and back into the world of 3D". I had to ponder this for a moment and reflect on what he was actually saying to me. My life is on a linear stretch of canal, surrounded by a 3D world of hills and valleys all waiting to be explored and yet here I am drifting in the murky waters of the Leeds to Liverpool canal. I can't argue with his point and it is a statement that will cling to me like sticky buds to cloth in the height of summer. But for now I chose not to pick at it.

My financial situation has not improved but my soul has connected to something way bigger than me and in this I find peace. I do not know what the future holds, but I know this much is true; I have experienced life in a way that feels like a ferocious scribble on a page. There is often no rhyme or reason to the movement of the lines, but when you look closely there are misshaped pockets of light just waiting to be coloured in. My rainbow pencils hold a spectrum of colour and only I can hold them and make the magic happen. I pick one up and start to draw.

The End.

Acknowledgements

A genuine thanks to Biddy Unsworth for taking the time to proof read 18 Months and for the encouraging words which followed.

My boys will always be an inspiration and I'm forever grateful of their spirit, which keeps me grounded at all times.

Finally, a thank you to friends and family who encouraged me to write and had confidence in my ability, you know who you are!

About the Author

Claire grew up on the edge of the Yorkshire Dales with humble beginnings. Her working class roots of being raised in a single parent family on an average council estate was one of the driving forces when seeking belonging and self-worth. The odds were stacked from a young age, with a general mantra that 'the most she could expect is to be pregnant at 16 and get her own council house.' The journey to break the stigma and low expectations has been a lifelong battle, with inner peace only being found in recent years.

Claire continues to drift on the Leeds to Liverpool Canal, she is a mother to her boys, a true friend to a select few and an acquaintance to many.